How to Be a Millionaire

Millionaire

Transform Your Life to Be Rich

Oscar Davis

ISBN – 13: 979-8-5503-5171-0

Table of Contents

Introduction

Congratulations on purchasing *How to Be a Millionaire,* and thank you for doing so. Money has not had a positive image in this world for the longest time. Phrases like, "money is the root of all evil," "money does not buy happiness," or "money causes greed," seem to dominate the conversations. Many people in society also see the attainment of wealth as evil or selfish. They wonder why one person has so much, while others have so little. When an individual has a goal to become a millionaire, they are seen as wealth hoarders.

The truth is money does not have to be a negative presence as long as it's not used for evil purposes. This is ultimately dependent on the person who gains wealth. Therefore, becoming a millionaire can be a blessing for you and anyone you are able to help. There are many different ways to become a millionaire, and the focus of this book will be on how to become one yourself. There are many opportunities out there to gain financial wealth, but you must understand how they work. Unfortunately, there are many cons out there that take advantage of people and their naivety. My goal is to provide legitimate action steps to help you earn your first million dollars and beyond.

Many of the techniques I learned came from the mind of the great financial expert, Ramit Sethi. I gained a lot of knowledge from Mr. Sethi, whom I consider a mentor, and I am excited to pass on the information to you. I am looking forward to teaching you how to be a millionaire and live a life of financial independence. The end result of money is not status, but freedom.

The following chapters will discuss the many blessings that come from being rich. There are plenty, and it's hard to deny that life is not at least easier when your finances are in order. The old adage of "money does not buy happiness, but it's easier to cry in a Mercedes than a broken-down sedan" will become apparent here. The focus of this book will not so much be budgeting but gaining wealth to the point where you don't have to skimp. When you do become a millionaire, I want you to be able to enjoy your newfound wealth because saving your money until you die is no fun at all. Having money also gives you the opportunity to be more generous. This is where others benefit from you being financially well off.

Furthermore, I will discuss the idea of debt and what the most common sources of crippling debt are. Useless debt can impede your ability to become rich, so it needs to be dealt with accordingly. Avoiding debt in the future is also important. Once we establish paying off the money that you owe, then I will discuss how to grow new money through various channels. An important factor is what you do with your money once you have earned it. Putting them in the right types of accounts is essential for increasing your wealth and limiting unnecessary fees. People who are rich have control of their finances.

Finally, I will discuss ways to save and invest money on a monthly basis while still being able to buy the things you want. Once again, if you have money, then enjoy it. You earned it, and it's your right to do so. Many people get caught up in all of their expenses that they have nothing left at the end of the month or go further into debt. Managing major expenses in the most stress-free way possible will be the final topic of this book. Overall, you will learn to master your money and become the millionaire you deserve to be. It won't be easy, but it will be worth it to become financially independent.

Thank you again for choosing this book on such a hot subject, as there are many others that cover similar topics, as well. We have made every effort possible to fill it with beneficial information you can start using today. We hope you enjoy it!

Chapter 1

The Blessings of Being Rich

Becoming rich is not a curse, nor is it evil. Money makes the world go round, as the expression goes, so the more of it you have, the better it is for your own world. There is plenty of money out there to go around, but the people willing to work for it are few. By the end of this book, you will be one of them. The focus of this chapter will be to discuss the blessings of being rich, and there are plenty of them.

When you learn to use your money properly and in a good way, you will always be able to look yourself in the mirror and know that you lived according to your moral standards. Some people will still believe you are evil, no matter how much good you bring to the world, but you can't please everyone. The goal here is to understand the blessings of money, embrace them, and share what you can with others. With great power does come great responsibility, as a certain superhero would say, and there is no denying that money brings power.

The Mindset of a Millionaire

Before any of us can become millionaires, we must develop the mindset of one. Yes, there is a way of thinking that rich people utilize in order to obtain and maintain their wealth. Many individuals don't possess the proper mindset, which is why they either never become rich or lose it once they gain it. Think about how many stories you've heard of people winning the lottery and then not showing any signs of it a few years down the line. If you don't think like a millionaire, you won't live your life like one. In this section, I will go over some ways to develop the mindset of a wealthy person. Once you see these, it will illustrate to you how much our thoughts influence our lifestyles.

Have a Vision

If you want to be a millionaire, you have to have a clear vision about what you want. Unless you win the lottery, inherit something, or fall into money by accident, somehow, then you will never become financially wealthy unless you can picture yourself in that manner. Also, you cannot simply chase money, but the idea of what your life will be like when you obtain it. Will you own a big house, own a large business, have a lot of cars, not have to worry about a job anymore, or be traveling around the world? Have a vision for what your life will be like as a millionaire, and always keep this in your thoughts. When you can imagine your life clearly, then it is easier to obtain. In this state, you don't necessarily have to know how you will achieve your picture-perfect life. You just have to know what it is.

Love What You Do

When you love what you do it, it does not feel like work, and you will put more effort into it. As a result, the money will follow. The reality is, going to work every day at a job you do not enjoy just to earn a paycheck will not make you a millionaire. You may need to do this for a short time period, but the goal is to move from this lifestyle and start building one you enjoy.

As you are working on your goal towards your dream career and situation, make the most of what you have at the moment. Shift your thought process, so you do not constantly bemoan your circumstances but start seeing the good in them. For example, your job is providing you income for your current lifestyle. It allows you to pay your bills, provide comforts for your family, keep shelter, and have food to eat. All of this is nothing to take lightly, and if people just looked at in this manner, they would realize that having a not-so-perfect job is much better than not having a job at all.

I also want you to start thinking about the things you like about your job. It does not matter how small it is. You can like your coworker, the fact that you help people every day, are making your company grow, or enjoy eating in the cafeteria. Pick out the little things you enjoy and turn them into big things. Once you determine what you like, start telling yourself that you love them. Speak life into your current situation and start cherishing what you have. The famous phrase of "you don't know what you've got till it's gone" is extremely relevant here. If you ignore the little joys, you will soon realize they are the big ones once they're gone.

Be Solution-Focused

Live your life by focusing on solutions instead of problems. Remember that what your mind perceives, your life achieves. This means that whatever you focus on regularly is what you will attract. This relates to the Law of Attraction, which I will cover more later on. Slowly, you will train your mind to start coming up with solutions immediately, despite what your circumstances are. You will then develop the millionaire's mindset of knowing that every problem can be overcome, no matter how big. The reason people become rich and then stay that way is that they don't quit when the going gets tough. When an obstacle arises, they look for ways to get over them as quickly as possible, and when they have a vision in mind, they never lose focus on that.

The truth is many things will happen that are beyond your control. This will never stop and might even increase as you go after more wealth. Being solution-focused will bring you a positive mindset that allows you to over problems much more efficiently. Many individuals do not reach financial wealth because they give up so easily. An obstacle comes up, and they see it as a sign of not going after their dreams. Instead, use these blocks that come up as a gauge to see how serious you are about your goals. Millionaires become excited about challenges because they know that treasures will exist on the opposite side.

Think about this for a moment. How often is there a beautiful view right in front of you. In many cases, you have to travel long distances or climb a great mountain to view them. However, once you do, you realize the destination was completely worth it. Have this same thought-process when going after your millions. There will need to be a lot of effort that gets put in, but once you achieve your goal, the results will be nothing but sweet.

Don't Take Things Personally

Millionaires do not take things that happen to them as an attack towards their character in any way. Instead, they accept everything as a learning experience, whether it is success or failure. People who are rich do not celebrate victories for too long and don't dwell on defeats either because they realize both are short-lived.

Take Risks

You will never become rich if you do not learn how to take risks. Do your research, learn what you can, and consider the risk-to-rewards ratio. After that, it is up to fate because there is only so much we can control in life. You must learn to take chances in order to reach the next level. Once you reach that level, you will need to continue taking risks.

Now, I am not telling you to jump into things foolishly. The risks you take must be educated. For example, if you want to go skydiving, then you need the proper equipment and training. The same goes for building your wealth. You must develop a plan and then have the courage to execute it.

Look for ways to Help Others

This may sound counterintuitive, but millionaires actually give more to others than they take in. This is because they offer a service of some kind that the public will benefit from. Look for ways to provide for others, and you will get plenty back in return.

Become Growth-Oriented

The reason millionaires gain and then keep their wealth is because they are always trying to grow in some way. They realize that the growth process is never-ending and is needed to continually amount their riches. The best way to achieve this is to never stop learning. Millionaires thirst for knowledge every day, and if they don't learn something constantly, they feel empty inside. You must also never stop learning if you want to develop a millionaire's mindset.

Why It's Okay to Spend Money

You have probably been told many times in your life to save every penny and stop wasting your finances on materials you will never need. Yes, it's true that if you spend everything you earn and never save or invest, you will lose everything and go into debt. However, why do we feel the need to go towards the extreme in these situations? What is the point of having money if you cannot enjoy it? We all work hard to make an income, whether it is from a job, running a business, or making investments. Why is it wrong to spend this money on the things you enjoy? Are we all supposed to make millions of dollars and then hoard it until we die? Sure, we can pass it off to our family, but then are they not allowed to enjoy it either?

I don't know about you, but I want to have some fun with my millions, and you should feel the same way. Become okay with spending your money and having fun. If you can afford it, then go for it because it is your money. No one has the right to tell you how to spend it, and you should never be ashamed of enjoying your wealth. We have one life to live, so let's start living it. Buy that cup of coffee at the café, eat at your favorite restaurant, go on that vacation, and buy that sports car that you love.

The goal is to create a spending plan based on your income. I am certainly not telling you to spend your entire paycheck or source of income. You must use a certain amount of money to help you grow more. However, never feel that you can't have fun in life. There are many things in life that you can experience, and you need money to do them. A spending plan allows you to focus on expenses that you need and really want. On many occasions, we will buy things that will bring instant gratification but bring no long-term value. Be mindful of these expenditures because it really is just like throwing money away.

If you buy a guitar, for example, and never use it, then it was a totally worthless expense. I cannot tell you not to buy this guitar, but I will suggest that the money can be used for something that will actually be useful in some way. For instance, buying a sports car and then being able to ride around town while enjoying it is a useful expense. It is bringing you great joy.

One thing you want to avoid is developing a consumer's mindset. Buy goods and services is great for the economy and opens up jobs for people. A restaurant that gets a lot of business needs to hire more employees. However, if you only focus on consuming, then you will become addicted to shopping and eventually spend all of your money. When your money is gone, then you will go into debt to buy more. It becomes a vicious cycle.

Do not try to keep up with the Joneses. I urge you not to buy things because other people have the item. In this regard, you are not purchasing an item because you want to. You just want to show other people up and make them envious of you. This does not bring you joy. True happiness comes from within and not from the validation of other people. You don't need others to praise you constantly. Your success will speak for itself. Never try to keep up with anyone, whether it's friends, family, neighbors, or perfect strangers.

Also, never allow people to guilt-trip you about the way you live. Often, people who are close to us will try to bring shame by pointing out the things we do not have.

As a result, we feel bad for ourselves and then try to get a hold of that item. Do not fall for their trap. There are people who will always have more than you in terms of material possessions. Do not worry about them and just focus on you.

"Too many people spend money they earned, to buy things they don't want, to impress people they don't like."

-Will Rogers

Will Rogers speaks a lot of truth in the above statement. When you do make purchases in your life, ask yourself the following questions:

- How does spending money on a specific item affect my life? It does not have to be anything business-related. It should just add some type of value. For example, if you buy a cup of coffee every morning from a café because it is delicious and soothes your soul, then that is a legitimate reason to buy that coffee.
- Where can I stop spending money and not feel like something is missing from my life? Going back to the coffee example, if you get the same joy from a homemade cup of coffee as you would from a café, then perhaps that purchase is not necessary.
- Am I spending money on items that I could find somewhere else and not reduce the quality of said purchase?
- In terms of what I spend my money on, what do hold the most value on?

These questions will help you determine your priorities when it comes to purchasing things. The point here is that you must never feel guilty about spending money you have worked hard to earn. If someone is not supporting you financially, then you do not have to listen to their criticisms about your spending habits. It is that simple. So, when you start bringing in that cash, be ready to have some fun with it too. With all of that being said, here is a quick rundown of why you should have fun with the money you bring in.

- It was earned by you. Making money takes effort, no matter what people tell you. You must work hard for it, whether physically, mentally, or both. Enjoy the fruits of your labor. Just don't put yourself in a tight spot.
- You have the money to do so. Yes, I urge you to not go into debt for your expenses, but if you have your finances covered, then take some of that extra cash and enjoy some of the finer things in life.
- Spending money on things you enjoy can be a blast. Those of us who are meticulous savers know that feeling of watching our bank accounts grow. However, getting to experience something we love can bring us many thrills. It is important to find a balance between spending and saving. Remember, you cannot take money to the grave.
- You make a lot of memories. I really don't hear people recalling great memories of walking into a bank or seeing money gets direct-deposited into their accounts. Memories some from having great experiences, and on many occasions, these experiences require money. I just can't imagine a situation where putting money into a savings account would bring the

same memories as sitting on a beach in your favorite location, going on a new adventure, or buying your dream car. Start making those memories.

- Time is way more precious than money. You can always figure out a way to make money, but once time has passed, it can never come back. It is impossible to live the same day over again, so be more focused on spending your time wisely than about money.

Being Cheap can be a Bad Thing

You may think that being frugal, or a cheapskate, only harms you; however, it can impact other people, as well. Of course, they will not feel it nearly as much you do. At least, not in the direct sense. You may have always been taught that being cheap is the smart way to live life. This may not always be the case, though. Being thrifty can be beneficial in specific moments, but at other times, it can be harmful. There is also a fine line between being a cheapskate and a conscientious spender. The following are some ways that taking the less expensive route can create more damage.

It Can Be Bad for Your Health:

People often choose cheaper food as a way to save money. Healthier culinary options can hit the pocketbooks in a way that makes people uncomfortable. However, even if you don't pay a lot upfront for less expensive food, you might end up paying later down the line with your health. In many studies, people experience obesity at much higher rates when they avoided healthy food options because of the price. I do think it's a shame that a burger at a drive-thru can cost less than a salad, but that's the reality for now. Still, be willing to spend a little extra in his regard because the food you eat will have a massive impact on your well-being down the line.

Besides fast-food, meals that come in a can or packaging might be filled with preservatives and salt that can be devastating to your heart health. I know it's appealing to buy ten packets of ramen noodles for $0.15 each, or whatever the price is, but keep eating these, and that little amount of money will turn into a huge problem down the line. Opt for fresher meals that you can cook at home. Eating healthy is not as expensive as you may think and will be worth it to you in the end.

I am not asking you to become a health nut or anything. Healthy food that tastes good still exists. You can even make seemingly unhealthy options into healthier ones. For example, grilling a burger at home with fresh lean meat can be delicious and better for your health than a fast-food burger. The bottom line is, don't allow being cheap to negatively impact your health. Of course, it is definitely okay to splurge once in a while.

You Get What You Pay for:

It is great to get a deal on things like clothes, toys, furniture, and other personal items. However, these materials may also wear down quicker, causing you to make another purchase earlier than you anticipated. It might serve you well to buy higher quality products that will last substantially longer and avoid constant expenses over a certain period of time. For example, if you buy a blazer made from quality material and it lasts you several years, it is much more economical than having a cheap blazer wear down quickly and becoming useless. You get what you pay for. Always remember that.

This same concept holds true for services that are rendered. If you hire a contractor to perform work on your house, you cannot simply hire the cheapest one. Quality of work also matters, so if the person you get for a reduced price does shoddy work, then you will pay an exorbitant amount in the long run. Imagine taking your vehicle to a mechanic because he offered repairs for 25% less than the competition. As a result, not only did the actual problem not get resolved, but even more issues arose later on. All of these factors must be taken into consideration, or you will end up paying more in the end.

Of course, cheap does not always mean bad. There are certain lesser expensive options that can have the same, or more, benefits than the expensive ones. I just don't want you to have the mindset that cheaper is better. You need to do your research.

A Less Expensive Home can become more Expensive in the Long Run:

Yes, buying a home that is five, ten, 15, 20, or more ears older can save you on the initial down payment and the monthly payments. However, in the long run, older homes can cost you more in repairs. It is estimated that 3.95% of a home's value is spent on repairs by the average homeowner if it was built prior to 1970, versus 2.53% on a post-1999 home. Also, the monthly payment on a house that has a value of a few more thousand dollars will not be much higher.

You Might Get in Trouble With the Government:

People are hesitant to hire a tax professional, but when you are able to avoid an audit, that expensive accountant is worth their weight in gold. According to a 2014 statement, roughly 2.6 million people made errors in their math while doing taxes. As a result, about 1.7 million adjustment notices were sent out. Even a decimal location error can result in adding an immense amount of money to a tax bill. Hire a professional with a good record, and you can save a lot of heartache and pain in the future.

Being Cheap can Become Wasteful:

I am sure many of you have bought groceries in bulk because they were offering such a good deal. However, overbuying can also lead to being wasteful. For instance, if you buy an excessive amount of produce, but are not able to finish it, then it must be thrown away. You did not save money in this instance. You actually wasted it.

You Might Get Shortchanged on a Salary:

Being cheap actually affect how much money you end up making. The term "dress for success" does mean something. Hiring companies often view candidates wearing nicer and name brand clothes as more deserving of a higher salary.
Of course, if you can save money on something and not reduce the quality of the substance, then it's definitely in your best interest to go for cheap. Never become frugal to the point that you create a worse life for yourself.

Why it's Great to Be a Millionaire

There is no denying that money brings a certain level of happiness into our lives. We always hear the phrase that money does not make you happy. It is true that if you are a miserable person when you have no money, you will continue to be when you become rich. However, having wealth makes life easier to live in many respects. Think about how much less stress you have when you don't have to worry about your finances. Even having a small cushion in the bank can ease anxiety in a significant way. Being rich has its advantages, and the following are some of the main reasons it is great to be a millionaire.

You Have Financial Freedom

Financial freedom goes beyond having zero debt. It means you can manipulate your reality to a certain degree. By this, I mean that the more financial freedom you have, the less you have to do the things you don't want to. Money can expand your options and opportunities for personal and professional growth. You will be able to create more diversity in your life by traveling to new places, eating different types of food, meet a variety of people, and have experiences that most people can only dream about or have never heard of.

Better Crisis Management

While we can never avoid all crisis situations, being wealthy, and having financial resources can help us tremendously in managing these moments. The following are a few examples:

- If your car breaks down and needs a major repair, you can easily get it fixed, and if needed, buy a new car.
- Having financial resources to hire a good legal team can get you out of a lot of trouble.
- It is easier to escape areas of natural disasters.
- You can handle and pay for proper healthcare in emergencies.

You Can Bring Joy to those Around You

Having money allows you to show others a good time. When you can treat your friends or family to some great experiences, it makes you feel great inside. Imagine taking your parents to an island when they could never afford to leave their hometown. Imagine having friends come from out of town and dining them at some upscale restaurants. Imagine buying your parents a car, house, or funding their retirement. All of these things will make you feel good about yourself.

Perform Great Charity Work

Whatever you may think about rich people, there are many out there doing great work and helping the less fortunate. When you are financially wealthy, it gives you the ability to help others and donate to causes you believe in.

You Meet a Different Level of People

I spoke earlier about the mindset of a rich person. People who are financially wealthy think differently about the world and have likely experienced things that the average person has not. You will get to learn and understand these individuals and even become like them eventually.

Time to Study

When you are a millionaire, you have more time to study and learn new things without constant distractions. If you want to learn a new language, you can buy the courses. Even better, you can travel to the country and learn the language that way. Having financial wealth increases your ability to grow and learn.

Stop Saying "I Can't Afford That"

"I can't afford it," or a similar phrase, is a common answer when an individual finds something too expensive, whether it is a physical item, food, or a travel destination. Saying that you cannot afford something gets you off the hook for buying it, and you get to go on your merry way. The problem is over, and you never have to worry about it again. The only problem is you have completely closed off your mind to any possibility of growth. Saying that you can't afford something is essentially a cop-out. You are not giving yourself a chance.

Instead, start using the phrase, "how can I afford this?" This simple rephrasing opens up your mind and changes your thought processes. Instead of immediately becoming closed off, you give yourself a chance for growth. If you believe that you can't afford something, then you will never be able to. If you tell yourself you can someday, then you at least have some faith in your abilities. I will go over some of the main reasons why you should stop using this limiting phrase. This is the scarcity mindset all the way, which is the complete opposite of how millionaires think.

It Makes You a Victim

Saying that you cannot afford something makes you a victim because you are admitting that you are under the control of your finances. You are bonded to your money situation, and you have no way of getting out of it. Instead of automatically shutting yourself down when you see a price tag, ask yourself how you can do to afford that item. Can you work overtime at your job? Can you get a second job? Can you get a loan with a low-interest rate (for bigger purchases, like a house or car)? Can you borrow from a friend or family member? Can you sell something you don't need or want to get money for this purchase? These are all options you can come up with, but you won't if you don't give yourself a chance.

It Discourages You

When you use this type of negative and limiting language, it makes you lose any type of hope for success. You start wondering, "why even bother," because you have no faith in achieving what you desire. At least give yourself some choices, so you don't become discouraged so easily. Ask yourself what small changes you can make in your life so that that you can ultimately afford what you're going after. This will cause you to not feel trapped, and you will have some momentum moving forward.

It Puts You in a Comparison Mentality

Whenever we look at what someone else has and decide we can't afford it ourselves, then we compare our success to theirs and always fall short. We begin to feel like failures. Never compare yourself to anyone else.

Even if you can't afford what they have now, it does not mean you won't be able to in the future. Constantly focus on what you can accomplish, and don't worry about what other people are doing. You are not in competition with them.

Law of Attraction

It is important to go over the Law of Attraction because it is imperative to know what you are attracting from the universe. If you attract the wrong things with your way of thinking, then you will never become a millionaire. The Law of Attraction can be targeted towards any area of your life. The focus here will be on the attainment of wealth. The foundation of this law is that whatever your mind pays attention to is what the universe will give you. Even if you are thinking about something in a negative way, the fact that you are focused on it sends signals to the universe that you want it. For example, if your mindset is that you don't want to be poor, the fact that you are thinking about poverty will attract those circumstances into your life. Instead, shift your mindset towards thinking about riches. Picture yourself with millions of dollars, rather than an empty wallet.

You will need to take some active steps to make the Law of Attraction really start working for you in your life.

Single Out Your Limiting Beliefs about Money

To make the Law of Attraction work for you, you must identify and assess your limiting beliefs about money. This mindset has probably been ingrained in you since childhood since most Individuals play it safe when it comes to finances. This is also why most people do not obtain great wealth. They are far too limited and don't give themselves enough credit for the potential they have.

I want you to realize your potential and see that you are only bound by the limits you create. Once you assess and understand the boundaries related to money, then you can start seeing it for what it truly is. Money is accessible and unlimited. You just have to go after it. You will lose money, but that does not mean it is gone forever.

A great technique that many people use to address their limiting beliefs about money is to recite positive affirmations. An example can be, "When I go after money, it will come to me." These positive affirmations that you tell yourself will be the basis of what you attract.

Visualize Yourself Already Being Rich

I spoke about visualization earlier, but in regard to the Law of Attraction, if you are able to visualize your wealth as if it's already been achieved, then you are more likely to attract it. If you want to attract money, then visualize yourself already having it. Imagine looking at a bank statement with a large number that indicates how much money you want. This method can serve as a powerful motivating tool. In addition, it will create an abundance mindset instead of a scarcity mindset. You will recognize that money is out there if you are willing to go after it. The abundance mindset is easy to have once you are already rich, but it will serve you well to start shifting towards it now.

You will start to feel wealthier already. When the money starts pouring in, you will act as if you've already been there. The more you train your mind to think this way, the harder it will be to break the cycle. You will continue to have an abundance mindset as you are gaining your millions and then continue to achieve more.

The Universe Will Provide You with what You're Grateful for

Never underestimate the power of gratitude. The universe will provide you with more of what you're grateful for. Therefore, if you show gratitude for your earnings, no matter how large or small, the universe will recognize this and provide you with more.

I want to clear up a few things about the Law of Attraction that people find confusing. The law simply means you will attract what you think about. However, it does not negate the necessity for going after it. You will simply find more opportunities to achieve what your mind is processing. For example, if you are thinking about more money, it does not mean millions of dollars will suddenly fall out of the sky. It means more opportunities to earn money will present themselves. Remember that you will attract what your mind conceives. If you think about success, you will find more opportunities for success. If you think about failure, then that is all you will experience. Understanding the power of the Law of Attraction will benefit you greatly while becoming a millionaire.

What Ramit Sethi says about Money

I have made it no secret that Ramit Sethi has been a personal hero of mine when it comes to finances. I learned much of what I know by reading his works, and whenever I can drop some pearls of wisdom from the man himself, I will do so. Mr. Sethi is not shy about his views regarding money. Just like I stated about, he is opposed to living with the scarcity mindset. Instead, he wants people to live with a growth-oriented way of thinking.

When a financial expert told him to stop buying lattes, jeans, and other expensive items he enjoyed, he was confused. He was basically being told not to buy anything he doesn't need. With this thought-process, everyone might as well go live in a cage and never enjoy anything. Mr. Sethi did not believe in this. He believes that people should spend money on luxurious things they enjoy, while mercilessly cutting costs on the things they don't.

I love hearing his message, and the first time that I did, it completely changed my life and how I thought about money. Mr. Sethi notes that when he was more rigid in is expenses, he was less successful. This is because he did not allow his mind to open up to all of the possibilities in the world. Once he stopped worrying about how he could afford things, he found ways to make it happen.

The purpose of this chapter was to cover some of the theories and philosophies about wealth. I will now start going over concrete ways to get out of debt and increase your riches. You are well on your way to becoming a millionaire.

Chapter 2

Getting Past Debt

"The man who never has enough money to pay his debts has too much of something else."

Many people out there cannot even think about becoming rich because they are underneath the thumb of crushing debt. They have no idea how they'll get away from it, and the more they try to avoid it, the greater it becomes. The debt crisis is a serious issue for many people who end up living their lives, never getting out of it. This can be due to poor financial decisions or having something unexpected occur, like a medical problem. Debt can rack up quickly before someone even realizes how far under they are. What makes it worse is are the high-interest rates that continue to add extra money, even if you don't spend anything.

The focus of this chapter will be to discuss the most common sources of crippling debt and what people can do to get over their financial issues. I will also go over ways to prevent going into debt in the future. The bottom line is that debt is money you have to pay back, and if you owe creditors a lot of money, then you will never truly be rich.

Sources of Debt

Debt accumulation can come from many different sources, and falling into it can feel like climbing out of a slippery cage with nothing to hold onto. I will go over the most common types of debt and some simple ways to get out of it. In some instances, debt can be a positive thing, like a mortgage or business loan. These types of debts can bring in some extra money. However, you still need to prevent them from getting out of control. There is nothing economical about a mortgage or business loan you cannot pay off.

Credit Card Debt

Credit cards have made our lives much simpler. We don't have to carry around cash or checks anymore. With the swipe of a card, a payment is made. We can even order things online and have them delivered to our house with ease. Unfortunately, all of this convenience has caused many people to go into credit card debt. Of course, the easiest way to avoid this financial issue is to not get into debt. However, if that ship has sailed for you, then there are some techniques to pull you out from under the water.

The first thing you need to do is determine how many credit cards you have, and the amount of debt owed on each one. Write these numbers down along with the interest rate for each card. From here, you have two options: Start paying off the amount you currently have due or call each credit card company and negotiate a lower payment. I will admit that some companies are more amenable than others, but most of them will try to work with you to a certain degree.

First of all, you want to establish a good rapport with your creditors, so they know you are trustworthy. If you are going to be late on a payment, then it's best to call in advance to let them know. If you are completely overwhelmed with your credit card debt, then there are a few settlement options you can explore, including:

- Asking them to move the payment date. For example, if your payment is due on the first of the month, then you can ask them to move it to the 15th.
- Requesting a lower interest rate. This is a good option if you've been able to pay your bills on time up to this point.
- Having them reduce your payment for a short period of time.

If you need bigger concessions, your credit card issuer will likely cut off your credit until the debt is paid off. If you do need some extra help, then consider making the following requests:

- Asking for a forbearance agreement, or a period of time where you don't have to make payments.
- Setting up a long-term repayment plan with a reduced or zero interest option.
- Paying a lump-sum settlement at a reduced amount. For example, if you were going to end up paying roughly $10,000 over a year making monthly payments with a certain interest rate, then you might be able to ask for a lump-sum payment of $7,000 if you have the capital.

Depending on which area you need help with, you will have to speak to a certain individual at the credit card company. For instance, if you want to change your payment date, you can usually talk to anyone in customer service. On the other hand, if you want a reduction in your interest rate, then you will have to talk to someone in management. Whatever new agreement you make with your credit card issuer, make sure to always get it in writing. Unfortunately, you should never trust a person's word, especially when it comes to money. In addition, these companies are dealing with countless transactions, and you cannot expect them to remember everything without a paper trail.

Once you determined what you owe, calculate how long it will take you to repay everything back based on your monthly budget. You can find several payment calculators online, too, from sites like NerdWallet. Now, put your credit cards in order from highest to lowest interest rate and start paying them off in that order. You will save the most amount of money if you pay off the highest interest cards first. Some financial gurus advise you to pay off the credit cards with the lowest amounts on them first. This is an option, as well, but you might end up paying way more in the long run.

If you can only pay the minimum due every month, that's a good starting point, but try to increase this amount by a little bit each month. If you get paid twice a month, then you can put a little from each paycheck towards credit card payments and even make two payments each month. You will be surprised at how much quicker you will pay off your loans.

While paying of your credit card debt, steer clear of racking up more. Otherwise, you are defeating the purpose. Once you pay off your credit cards, you can start getting rid of some. I advise that you just have one credit card for everyday expenses. If you have a business, then you can have a separate one to track those expenses. Finally, have one available only for emergencies. Put it in a safe if you have to so you can avoid the temptation of pulling it out all the time.

Medical Bills

Medical bills are some of the hardest debts to avoid because you cannot always control getting sick or injured. Yes, you can take all the proper precautions, but life is unpredictable and can catch you off guard at any moment. With the cost of healthcare today, medical bills can add up quickly. Always comb through your medical bills to catch major errors. Was there anything they charged for that you did not receive? The people in the billing department at hospitals make mistakes too, so it's important to catch them. Medical billing errors can cost you thousands of dollars if you are not careful.

After verifying that all services were done and accounted for, your next step is to negotiate your medical bills down. If this process is too overwhelming, then I suggest various resources to help you. These include:

- Government programs like Medicare and Medicaid Savings Programs.
- Advocates for medical bills
- Medical bill consolidation
- Ask your hospital about payment settlement options. Evidence of financial hardship may have to be given.
- Ask for help from local churches, support groups, and charity organizations.
- Crowdfunding sites can be a great option for getting donations from family, friends, and even generous strangers. GiveForward and GoFundMe are examples of sites like these.

Mortgage

Buying a home can be an exciting time, but also an expensive debt. If you are not careful, you can get behind on your payments quickly and end up losing everything. When you buy a home, always make sure you have a comfortable cushion left over for repairs and other unexpected expenses. Do not plunk everything and more into the down payment. Once you move in, I suggest being a couple of months ahead on your payment. Meaning you have paid your mortgage several months out. For example, if it's August, you already have everything paid through November 1st. This provides an extra cushion, so you will be safe for a little while without needing to make a payment if needed. Of course, never deplete your emergency account by doing this.

If you are struggling to make your mortgage payments for whatever reason, then certain options do exist for you. Here are a few suggestions for reducing your monthly mortgage payment:

- Refinance your mortgage to get a reduced interest rate. Your interest rate can add quite a bit to your mortgage payments, so even reducing it by 1-2% points can be beneficial.
- Some individuals obtain primate mortgage insurance, or PMI when they first get the loan so they can pay a reduced down payment. Once you own 20% or equity in your home, then it's important to get rid of this insurance. Otherwise, you will have an unnecessary addition to your payments.
- Extend the timeline on your loan. While this will increase the amount of time to pay and cause you to pay more in the long run, it will reduce

your monthly payment, which can help tremendously if you're in a bind. Even with the extended schedule, you can still pay your previous payment amount if you can afford it. It's a win-win in this situation.

- Many mortgage payments include property text. While you cannot get rid of those if your county requires them, you can get a new assessment on your home and reduce your property taxes. Only do this if you know your home has lost value. If your property has gained value, then your property taxes might go up if you get a new assessment.

Just like with any other debt, make it a goal to pay off your mortgage as quickly as you can based on what you are able to afford. Even putting a couple extra hundred dollars towards your principal balance can help pay off the loan more efficiently.

Student Loans

Higher education can be beneficial for many people and help them achieve their dream careers. Unfortunately, every few families can afford a college or university education, so student loans must come into play. After four years, and even more, if you get a graduate education, the money really adds up and can become overwhelming. Many individuals work their whole lives paying off their student loan debt. Imagine having to pay for the money that you borrowed 30-40 years ago. Some people don't have to imagine this because it is a reality for them.

College is not getting any less expensive, which means loan amounts are going to increase. There are a few precautions you can take to avoid loans. First of all, determine if college is necessary for the particular career path your choosing. While some professions do require a college degree, there are several great options, like trade schools, that are much less expensive. In some cases, you can even get training on the job.

If college is necessary for you, it is still possible to circumvent massive debt by doing some preplanning. Consider some of the following options:

- Scholarships: There are many types of scholarships out there, and they are usually based on academic performance or financial need. Never eschew any scholarship amount because having a whole bunch of small scholarships can add up. Fastweb is a great search tool to help you find scholarships you are eligible for.
- Grants: These are similar to scholarships but usually awarded through the government or certain organizations. Federal Pell Grants are a common type of government grant.
- Work-Study Programs: With this route, you work part-time through work which is arranged by the Federal Work-Study Program. Any earnings you receive get shifted towards your educational payments.
- Before matriculating into college, consider working for a little while to save up some extra money to live off. While in school, work part-time if you can and use vacation time to work a little extra.

Of course, all the above options are to avoid taking out loans in the first place. If you are already struggling with student loan debt, then there are a few options to help you get out from under them. Public service loan forgiveness strategies and volunteering to forgive educational charges can be great options for reducing student loan debt. Just like with the other debts, once you determine how much you need to pay, calculate how long it will take you based on interest rates and your monthly budget.

Deferring or postponing your student loan payments is an option if you can't afford your payments at the present moment. This will, at least, buy you some time to get your financial affairs in order. Continuing your education, unemployment, and military service are just a few situations that allow you to take a deferment.

There are also income-based repayment plans that can help you. If your monthly student loan payments are a significant enough portion of your income, then you are likely to qualify for this assistance.

Do not just assume you are stuck with your debt with no options for assistance. There are many ways you can get help, and any type of reduction in loans or payment amounts can be beneficial. Seek out help if you need it, and you will find someone to assist you. Debt can be a scary and overwhelming process. If you have no idea how to get out from underneath it, then don't try to go at it alone. It may take a while to pay off everything you owe, but slowly bring down that debt without adding anything new, and you will slowly get yourself caught up.

If things become really bad, there are options for bankruptcy and loan settlement, but these can wreak havoc on your credit, which will take years to get over.

Really do your research and even speak to an attorney, credit counselor, or financial advisor who is an expert in these areas.

Dealing With Collectors

Believe it or not, many people have a sour impression about debt collectors because of stories they have heard or what they have seen in movies. However, even though it can be intimidating dealing with these individuals, there are certain rights you should be aware of. These fall under the Fair Debt Collection Act, which prevents collectors from bullying you with abusive, unfair, and even deceptive practices. While these individuals have to be persistent, it is illegal for them to harass you. Your credit cards, mortgage, student loans, and medical bills are covered under this act, but business debts are not.

Debt collectors can call, send emails, text, or send letters to collect money that is owed to them. There are limits to these methods, though. They cannot contact you at inconvenient times or places. For example, they cannot meet you at your house or while you are shopping. They also cannot call you before 8 AM or after 9 PM without your consent. Finally, they cannot call you while at work unless they have permission.

A debt collector cannot discuss your debt with anyone else unless it is your spouse. Also, if you are being represented by an attorney, they can speak with them. A collector is allowed to call people who know you to get a phone number or address, but they can usually only call that person once.

Whatever practices a debt collector will follow, always remember that they can't harass, lie, or treat you unfairly. You have the right to be treated with respect. Overall, I advise you to work with the debt collector the best you can and develop a relationship with them. Hiding and providing wrong information will only make the problem worse.

Consolidating Your Loans

It is easy to become stressed out when you are dealing with multiple payments at the same time. It can make you feel like your debt amount is larger than it actually is. Debt consolidation is an effective method for managing debt that works by rolling all of it into a single monthly payment. This can also lower your interest rate and give your credit score a little boost. Some ways to consolidate your debt is to take out a personal loan from a bank, credit union, or other financial institution, transferring payments from multiple credit cards into a single credit card, or using a home equity loan. This process provides many advantages for you.

- The most obvious benefit is that it turns multiple payments into a single payment. Having one large debt, versus five or six smaller debts is much easier to manage. The debt still exists, but you will be able to focus on it better.
- By paying off multiple high-interest accounts with a single loan, your interest rate can become significantly lower. People don't realize how much their interest rate affects their monthly payments, but reducing it by one or two points can create a tremendous amount of savings.

- You will get a nice boost in your credit score, which will help in many of your financial matters in the future.
- Consolidating your debt into a single monthly payment will create less stress for you. You are essentially clearing up your clutter.
- You can pay back your loan and reduce your debt much quicker. Debt consolidation takes multiple variables into account, like income and credit score, when determining the length of the loan amount. As a result, the debt will have a shorter payback period.

How to Avoid Future Debt

After clearing up the debt you once owed, it is essential not to fall into that trap again. You don't want to fix your problems and then end up back in the same place. First of all, you need to fix some spending habits. Beyond that, you can use the following tips to remain debt-free, or at least control your debt for the rest of your life. What I mean by controlled debt is having a mortgage or car payment that you can easily afford every month.

If You Cannot Afford it Without a Credit Card, Do Not Buy it

I want all of you to be able to afford luxury items that you enjoy. However, I also want you to use the money you have now to make these purchases. If you cannot buy something without a credit card, then you cannot afford it. Use cash whenever possible, or at least a debit card, so you avoid falling into the trap of putting everything on a credit card. Even the small items add up, and suddenly, you will end up with thousands of dollars that you owe.

Have Emergency Savings

Always have emergency funds that you can fall back on in case of an emergency. Most financial experts advise having about six months of your salary saved up for "just-in-case" situations. These funds are to only be accessed for real emergencies and not general purchases. As long as you have this saved up, have some fun with your money. You deserve it.

Always Pay off Credit Card Balances

The best way to avoid credit card debt is to never allow a balance to stay on your card. Therefore, whatever you charge every month, pay off in full. You can even make two payments in a month to make it more manageable for you. If you use your credit cards to earn rewards, then pay it off within a couple of days, or as soon as the balance hits.

Avoid Cash Advances with Credit Cards

Using your credit card so you can have cash on hand is an indication that you don't have control over your finances. The APR is higher than regular purchases, and you will likely be charged a fee. Check out other loan options, especially those that are interest-free, if this is a necessity.

Don't Carry too many Cards

I spoke about consolidating loans earlier. This goes along the same lines. Do not open too many credit cards to the point you can't keep track of your spending and bills. If you can get away with one card, then use those only.

Do This When Your Income Increases

People have a tendency to start spending more money right away after their wages go up. While I want you to enjoy your money, do not automatically start spending more. When you first get the pay increase, continue living like your old lifestyle until you save a little extra in the bank. After that, start enjoying your money more.

Your mind will be much more at ease when you are debt-free.

Having Proper Insurance

Insurance can be expensive, and people often wonder why they need it. Well, tragedies can strike at any time, and if you don't have insurance to protect your home, belongings, health, and even life, then you could be facing financial hardships at levels you have never experienced before. It is always better to have insurance and not need it, then not have it and need it. I will go over some common insurance types and how you can save on these services. Never believe that you can go without insurance. This is one area where you want to avoid taking a risk.

Homeowners Insurance

Homeowners' insurance is a necessity to protect your dwelling and everything that exists inside of it, include yourself. This is not a luxury item in any way. In fact, if your mortgage company learns that you don't have insurance, they will get some for you at a much more expensive rate. You will be paying, one way or another, so you might as well buy the insurance and get the best deal that you can.

Homeowners' insurance policies cover the interior and exterior of your home, the loss or theft of possessions, and personal liability in case someone gets harmed while on your property. Also, if your home becomes unlivable, for whatever reason, your insurance will cover the cost of a hotel or rental home while yours is being repaired. There will be daily limits here, so don't try to book a Ritz-Carlton, unless you can get a deal.

These types of policies are also customizable, based on the client's specific needs. For instance, if you are in a location that is prone to floods and other natural disasters, then you may need to tack on extra coverage for these situations. You ever know what might damage your home, so make sure you are protected in every way possible.

While insurances do exist to cover claims that are filed, they also exist to make money. Therefore, there are many factors that determine what your insurance rate will be. Some things might be well beyond your control, like the area you live in, while other issues you can manage. A significant factor in determining rates is how many claims you have filed in the past. My advice here is to reduce your number of claims by only using insurance when you have no other option. For instance, if you're deductible is $500, and a repair costs $550, then it will be to your benefit to just pay the extra $50 instead of filing a claim. This will help avoid skyrocketing your rates.

Another factor is the amount of coverage you want. Most insurance experts recommend a minimum of $300,000 worth of coverage. Of course, you can get these amounts for as low as $100,000. Determine how much coverage you need based on your home's value and what possessions you own. Remember, though, you can break your payment amounts down in monthly payments, so the sting of having to purchase extra coverage will not be as much. For example, if your insurance premium goes up by $100 annually, that's about eight or nine dollars extra each month.

Having a home security system does not only provide extra safety and peace of mind, but it can also reduce your insurance rates. Many insurance companies will view security as reducing the liability on your home. Therefore, your rate can be reduced, which might be enough to offset the monthly payments on the alarm system you set up.

Finally, you can always choose where you live. If you would rather live in a less liable area, which will lower your insurance rates, then consider this as an option. Once again, this depends on your mindset as far as where you want to live.

The bottom line is disaster can strike from anywhere and at any time. If your home and personal possessions get destroyed, or if someone gets injured while on your property, you could lose everything in an instant if you are not carrying insurance. Get the best rates you can by shopping around and talking to many different agents. Never feel like you have to buy a specific policy, so be aware of pushy insurance agents. Buying solid insurance now can save you a truckload of money down the line. It is an investment you cannot go without.

Auto Insurance

If you own a motor vehicle of some sort, then you need to be properly insured against accidents, injuries, thefts, and liabilities. You never know what can happen in life, and auto insurance will protect you and your vehicle, whether it is on the road or tucked away safely in your garage. Never use any type of excuse for not having insurance. If you can't afford it, then you can't afford a car, period!

There are many affordable options for car insurance based on how much coverage you want or need. The world is an unpredictable place. If and when tragedy strikes, you will be happy with the fact that you have car insurance. This type of coverage not only protects your car, but also protects you from getting sued, and will cover the expenses of the other driver if an accident is ever your fault. In addition, your car can get stolen or damaged in other ways. You will need insurance to bail you out during these times.

Health Insurance

Unless you live in a country where your medical bills are always covered, health insurance is an absolute necessity. Unfortunately, it can be hard to get inexpensive coverage when you add dental and vision to the plan. However, affordable options do exist out there. You just have to talk to the right agent.

Once again, don't assume you won't need medical assistance because you are young. First of all, even young and healthy people have been blindsided by unexpected illnesses. The human body is an unpredictable organism. Also, accidents and injuries can occur at any time. Your health won't protect you if you're walking down the street, trip, and break your leg.

Always make sure you are covered to the best of your ability, so you don't get ambushed by thousands of dollars in medical bills. If you ever need to cut out expenses from your life, never let health insurance be one of them.

Life Insurance

Life insurance exists so that your loved ones will have sufficient financial assistance in the case of your passing. While this type of coverage is not helping you directly, it will protect those you care about and make sure they do not go into financial ruin, especially if you are the primary breadwinner.

Many other types of insurance, like business, liability, or disability coverage, are also options you should look into based on what you do for a living. For example, if you work in healthcare, then having liability insurance is a necessity in case of errors that might occur at work. Insurance, as a whole, is there to protect you and everything you have worked for. All of your hard work can be wiped out in an instant because of a single tragedy. Don't get caught in this situation because you are not willing to invest in proper insurance coverage.

Setting Up a Budget

A large part of avoiding debt is to set up a budget or plan for your finances. I am not asking you to track every penny. That will just get exhausting and ultimately become a timewaster. However, a simple budget should be set up so you can determine the direction of your money. Mainly, how much is going out and how much is coming in. You can also determine where the money is going out and what sources of income are bringing it in. The following are some steps to set up a budget for you, so you can better manage your money.

- Determine your total income amount. Start by calculating how much you make after taxes each month. An average is okay if your pay varies each month. Add in the rest of your income that you bring in from business, side hustles, part-time work, investments, alimony, or child support, etc. Any income should be added in, and once again, an average is okay if it varies every month.
- Calculate your expenses. Break them down into sections, like housing, utilities, food, and transportation. Getting an average of your expenses is okay. A common method is to take the amount you calculated, and then add 10% on top of it to account for unforeseen or unaccounted for expenses. For example, if you calculate your expenses to be $2,000 per month, then add 10% on top of that to make it $2,200.
- Now, calculate the difference and determine how much more your income is than your expenses. Hopefully, it is significantly more.
- Now, determine what you will do with your savings every month, whether it's increasing your expenses, investing, donating, or putting more towards savings. Determine how much room you have to splurge and go from there.

- Make this a habit. Assess your budget on a monthly basis and make sure you are keeping your head above water.

I want to fill you in on something. Making a budget is not just about making sure you are saving enough. It is also about making sure you have enough money to buy the things you want! When you are looking at your expenses, look at the items you buy simply for enjoyment, and assess whether you still want them. If you do and can afford them, then keep going. If not, then get rid of that expense and transition that money towards the things that actually bring you joy.

A lot of financial experts will tell you to start decreasing your expenses. I won't be telling you that. Instead, focus on the income area and figure out how you can increase the amount of money you bring in every month so you can continue to live with your current expenses and eventually buy even more of what you want.

A Budgeting Story

An elderly gentleman once called into a radio show with a financial expert. He had saved money his whole life, barely spent anything on fun, and was now in his early 60s. The gentleman asked the financial expert if it was okay for him to go on a cruise that his wife was planning that would cost roughly $5,000. The gentleman also informed the financial that he had about 1.5 million dollars saved up between all of his accounts, and all of his bills were paid off, including the house and car. Based on his budget, he was bringing in a couple of thousand dollars a month and saving at least 80-90% of it.

The financial expert told him, "No, it is not okay for you to go on this cruise." After some silence, the financial expert continued, "I want you to get a refund immediately and then purchase a cruise for at least twice as much and twice as long. If you enjoy it, then try to go on another one as soon as possible. Start enjoying yourself a little bit. You've definitely earned."

It was hard to gauge how the gentleman really felt because he seemed to be in a state of shock. Nonetheless, his mindset is common amongst so many people. They are terrified of spending money that even when they have such a strong cushion, they still can't bring themselves to have some fun and splurge once in a while. I am not sure what this elderly gentleman did after hanging up the phone, but I hope he followed the financial expert's advice.

If you want to deal with your debt, then you cannot ignore it. It will just make things worse. Instead, I want you to face it head-on and work actively to abolish it. Then, I want you to take active steps to make sure you don't drown financially ever again. It will take a lot of effort and discipline, but you can definitely do it.

"There is a limit to how much you can cut but there is no limit to how much you can earn."

-Ramit Sethi

Chapter 3

Setting Up the Right Accounts

You have probably heard countless stories of people who made millions of dollars throughout their careers and then ended up completely broke and even in debt. Whether it was a professional athlete, celebrity, entrepreneur, or someone who won the lottery, if they did not handle their money properly, then they ended up with nothing in the end. There are countless times where people end up filing bankruptcy or even committing tax fraud. Where did their money go? That is anyone's guess. What we do know is that they had no clue what was coming in and what was going out. If they did, nothing was done to make improvements.

Becoming rich is not just how much money you make but how much you can keep and grow. If you make $100,000 a year but spending $120,000, then you are actually making a negative $20,000. If you continue with your current habits, even if you somehow increase your salary to $200,000, you will still be in the hole. The focus of this chapter will be on what to do with your money once you have it in your possession. I won't be giving specific financial or stock advice. However, I want you to know your options to keep your money secure and grow steadily. Most rich people did not obtain their wealth overnight or with one step. Instead, they made small money moves that added up to make big changes. Let's talking about securing and growing your money.

Some Good Accounts

Back in the day, people would just open general savings and checking accounts and stash all of their money there. While this is better than doing nothing, there are other options available in the present time. In this section, I will go over some great financial accounts where you can safely put your money and grow it at the same time. Now, this is not going to make you a millionaire by itself. It will just steadily move you in the right direction.

Regular Savings Account

These are general accounts that offer a safe place to stow your money and little else. You will get very minimum growth as most accounts like these offer only a 0.01% annual interest rate. So, if you have $1,000 in the account, that's about a one-dollar annual return. These accounts can work well if you want to put money in and take it out whenever because there is usually no removal feel. There may be limitations on monthly transfers, though.

Standard Checking Account

Your regular checking account is what you should be using to pay bills and make everyday purchases. You should have a little bit of cushioning in this account for unexpected expenses, but the majority of your money should be placed in other types of accounts. Mainly the ones with higher interest rates. The best checking accounts offer minimal fees, a broad network of ATMs, and low minimum balance requirements. Many checking accounts only require a $25 minimum.

Money Market Deposit Accounts

These are offered by most banks and generally require a minimum initial deposit amount, like around $1,000. This minimum amount needs to be maintained; otherwise, fees will incur. There is also a limit on monthly transactions. These accounts usually offer a higher interest rate than a regular savings or checking account, but less than many other high-yielding accounts. The cash is pretty accessible in liquid funds if needed, but I advise not removing money from these accounts unless absolutely needed. Use standard checking or savings accounts for that.

High-Yield Savings Account

These generous accounts offer a higher interest rate than standard savings accounts and are still FDIC insured. The reason for the higher interest rate is that it requires a larger initial deposit. The access to the funds is also limited compared to a standard account. There are many high-yielding savings account types, so see which one you can have access to with the highest interest rates. Many banks offer these accounts to their loyal customers, so it's beneficial to develop a relationship with your banking institution.

Certificates of Deposit (CDs)

Most banks and credit unions offer these. These accounts offer high-interest rates, especially with larger deposits. The major catch with CDs is that you must leave the money there for a certain amount of time; otherwise, penalties can incur. For example, you can lose up to three months of interest. If you open a CD, expect to leave your money in there for the long haul and keep making regular deposits. Do not remove the money unless it is an absolute emergency. CDs are great ways to save up money for major purchases down the line, like a house or college for your children.

The benefit of all of these accounts is that they are risk-free. The money sits in the accounts and grows steadily. Since the accounts are FDIC insured, your money is well-protected.

Investment Accounts

A certain amount of your money should go into investment accounts, which are higher risk but also offer greater returns. Investment accounts can be opened at most banks and financial institutions. You can always speak with a financial expert at these locations to see what your best options are. The following are some good investment accounts where you can place and build up your wealth. Remember, while these offer a small amount of risk, growth can never occur without taking some chances.

Stocks and Bonds

Stocks and bonds are two separate trading options to look at. Each one offers its own advantages. A stock is when you have a stake of ownership in a company. These holdings are known as shares and vary in price based on the company's value. Stockholders are actually part owners in a publicly-traded company, and ownership amount is decided by percentages of shares held. Due to the nature of the market, stocks are higher risk and more volatile than bonds in the short term. Investors could lose a significant amount of money overnight. However, long term, stocks are usually much more valuable because of the potential for growth.

A bond is a company-owned debt or entity that is entered into with an investor. A bond investor earns capital through interest that is paid on the debt. Basically, they are considered IOUs which must be repaid in full, along with the interest payments. A private company, entity, or government creates bonds when capital is required to finance a new project, or some type of needed growth or development. Instead of creating loans through a bank, they pursue the help of investors. Bonds are lower risk than stocks because they are fixed-income investments, but do not provide nearly the same amount of growth and returns.

You can invest in stocks and bonds individually or with financial institutions through various security or investment accounts. I will go over some of these here.

Roth IRA

This is an individual retirement account where you get taxed on the money you put in, and all future withdrawals become tax-free. These are great for when your taxes will be higher during retirement than current times. You cannot contribute to a Roth IRA if you make too much money. As of 2020, the income limit is $139,000 for singles and $206,000 for married couples. The deposit limit is $6,000 annually if you are 50 or under and $7,000 dollars if you are over 50.

With an IRA, you can hold a combination of stocks, bonds, and cash based on your growth to risk ratio. This means that if you want more potential growth, you can have a higher percentage of stock holdings versus bond holdings. This will make your account riskier, as stocks can go up and down and do not offer steady growth like bonds.

Traditional IRA

Traditional IRAs are similar to Roth IRAs, but the contributions are pre-tax, so taxes will only be withheld when you withdraw funds. The tax amount will be whatever the income tax rate is at the moment. The annual limit on contributions is $6,000 if you are under 50, and $7,000 if you are 50 and over. The advantage that a traditional IRA will give you is that you can use contributions as a tax deduction.

In your account, you can hold a combination of stocks, bonds, and liquid cash holdings. Depending on how risky you want to be, you can hold a higher or lower percentage of stocks compared to bonds. Traditional IRAs are considered retirement accounts; therefore, it can be difficult to withdraw before the age of 59-1/2 without suffering immense penalties.

Mutual Funds

This type of fund's account is a popular and effective investment vehicle which can combine stocks, bonds, and various other securities. It can give individual investors access to diversified portfolios with relatively low fees. Mutual fund value depends on activity of the securities that are involved. Unlike buying individual stocks, mutual fund shares do not give the shareholders any voting rights. One share of a mutual fund represents many different stocks and securities.

The average mutual fund holds over 100 different securities, which provides a high amount of diversification. As a result, when a group of securities is doing poorly, the fund can make it up with others that are doing well. You will not feel losses and gains as strongly as you would with single securities.

Income in a mutual fund is earned through dividends on stock and interest on a bond. The investor generally has a choice of what to do with the earnings. They can either cash out and receive a check or have the money reinvested for continual growth.

Index Funds

A fund that consists of a diversified portfolio of securities like stocks or bonds that closely imitate the composition of specific financial market indexes. They have lower expenses and fees than actively managed funds and follow more of a passive investment strategy. The theory behind an index fund is that the market, as a whole, will outperform any single investment. Basically, instead of actively picking stocks and timing the market, the fund manager will build a portfolio of holdings that mirror the securities of a particular index, like the S&P 500. The index fund is a good low-risk retirement account.

401(k) and Other Company Retirement Accounts

A 401(k) is a type of company-sponsored retirement account that allows employees to contribute their pre-taxed income. Employers can match the contributions, too, allowing for extra growth. If your employer offers this type of benefit, then consider taking it. If you leave your employer, then you can often transfer your 401(k) to your new company. Other company retirement accounts include the 403(b), 457, and a SEP plan. The 401(k) can be broken down into a Roth and traditional style. Similar to the Roth IRA, transfers made to a Roth 401(k) will not be tax-deductible.

Buying Individual Stocks

Buying individual stocks from a brokerage firm can offer you more immediate growth, but less security. If one stock share goes down, you can end up losing a lot of money, especially if you own several shares. For example, if Amazon is trading for $2,000 per share, and you buy five shares, then you have $10,000 invested. If the price goes up to $2,500 per share, then you just made $2,500. If the share drops to $1,500 per share, then you lost $2,500. Some people like to time the market and sell at the highest points, but that is very unreliable.

To play the stock market in this manner, you will need to be very emotionally stable, because it can become a rollercoaster with the ups and downs in share prices. Playing the stocks is actually quite simple. You don't have to move to Wall Street to do it. Just use the following steps.

- Find an online stockbroker. After opening an account and transferring your funds, you can immediately start buying shares of different stocks based on your buying power. Some good online brokers include TradeStation, Charles Schwab, Fidelity, Robinhood, and Merrill Edge.
- Research the stocks you want to buy. Check out companies you already know from consumer experiences. Look at the company's annual reports, quarterly earnings, and recent news. Always remember that buying stocks comes with risks, so never invest more than what

you're willing to lose. There is no easy way to pick stocks.

- Decide how many shares you want to buy. This will directly relate to how much you can earn or lose. To get a feel for the company, you can start with one share and then build up from there.
- Optimize your stock portfolio by owning shares in companies you believe in and have researched well. Even the best investors have made blunders, so do not become discouraged.

This was just a quick rundown or different types of financial and investment accountments. To get more detailed information, you can always talk to a financial advisor.

The Power of Compound Interest

You may have heard of earning interest on your bank accounts. However, do you know the power of compound interest? This is the interest on a loan or deposit calculated on both the initial principal and the earned interest. For example, if your initial principal was $1,000, and your interest generates it to $1,005, then you will continue to earn interest on the $1,005 and so on.

The rate at which interest accrues depends on the frequency of the compounding periods. The following is the calculation for compounding interest.

- $\{P(1+i)^n - P\}$: "P" Correlates to the Principal amount; "I" constitutes the annual interest rate; "n" refers to the number of compounding periods.

Compounding interest can help you earn extra money on deposits but can be detrimental when taking out a loan. Ask your financial adviser about opening accounts with compounding interest rates.

Negotiate Your Way Out of Bank Fees

No matter how careful you are, fees can creep up on you, and you might even be penalized for a mistake you may or may not have made. Sometimes, it can be an oversight by either you or the financial institution. Fees are great for banks because they make a lot of money off of them. However, for the consumers and business owners, they can add up and become a major source of frustration. Lucky for you, many hidden fees can be waived or reduced with the correct approach. Remember, banks don't want to lose their clients either, especially the loyal ones. It is in your best interest to have a good relationship with your bank. You can also follow some of the tips provided in this section to convince your bank to drop their charges.

Investigate the Matter

Do not automatically become hot and bothered by hidden fees or charges. This could send you into a rage and cause you to explode on a banker. This is not fair to them either because they are likely just following the rules. A better option is to keep your cool and do some detective work. Assess what fees you are being charged, read up on the bank's rules, and compare the policies attached to different savings and checking accounts. Ask questions if you do not understand what is going on. This will help ensure no mistakes were made. If there was an error, being able to show how the fees don't align with the terms and conditions of the bank can help you avoid paying them.

Speak Up When Needed

It is your money that is being placed in a bank, so speak up about things you find unfair. Even if mistakes did not occur and the fees are appropriate, it does not mean you cannot question them in any way. It won't hurt you to see if your bank can waive these fees, or at least some of them. The worst thing they can do is say no, and then you can decide how to proceed from there. The institution might be willing to accommodate you, especially if the fee is new to you.

If you plan on negotiating, then it will behoove you to ask fast. Don't wait until you have been doing business with them for a while. After a while, your name could get added to the ChexSystem, which is a reporting bureau that collects information on those who did not pay their bank fees. This could create trouble for you later on. Investigate early and determine what your fees are. Then do your best to get out of them.

Visit the Bank In-Person

While it is convenient to do everything online and over the phone, there is still certain magic that in-person communication has. Negotiations usually turn out better when they are done face-to-face. That is because there is more of a personal interaction than email or phone. Facial expressions and body language will often give you more information over words alone. You can use this to gauge the conversation and switch gears if they are not reacting well to what you're saying. When the financial experts can see you in real-time, they might also have more empathy for what you need.

Keep it Classy

If you portray a bad attitude or speak negatively towards a person, they will not have much sympathy for you. This will make them less likely to help you, no matter what your story is. It is not about what you say but how you say it. Therefore, always keep it classy. When you are talking to someone on the phone, keep your voice friendly and professional. If you walk into a bank, remain poised, professional, and polite. If you sow them courtesy and respect, you are more likely to get it back.

It may benefit you to rehearse what you want to say. You can also get your frustrations out during these rehearsals, so you do not showcase them towards the staff at the bank. If you are communicating through email, write a few practices once to make your points concise, and get out your frustrations ahead of time.

Make an Open-Ended Request

Instead of asking concrete questions with a definitive yes or no answer, use open-ended questions to prevent shutting down the conversation immediately. For example, instead of asking, "Can I have my bank fees waived?" ask, "What options are available for me to reduce or waive my bank fees." Keep the questions open-ended, and it will keep the conversation moving. Even if you don't get exactly what you want, some concessions might be made.

Prove Your Point

Your sole reason for not paying your bank fees is that you simply don't want to. That's okay for a personal reason, but it probably won't make you any friends when using this line towards a banker. Nobody wants to pay bank fees, so come up with something better. Talk about your relationship with the bank, their great customer service, and how much you enjoy working with them. If you were charged a penalty and it was the first time, then you can explain that to the institution and bring up the fact that this was the first time you did something to get penalized for. Financial institutions will often have sympathy and understanding for a first-time offense.

Here is a common scenario that can occur: An individual pays with their joint debit card, thinking they have a certain amount in their checking account. However, they did not realize their partner had made a major charge the day before, so they accidentally overdraft their account. As a result, they are charged an overdraft fee. After realizing this, the individual calls the bank, explains to them what happened, takes responsibility, and then asks for any options for assistance as this was the first offense. The institution recognizes the client as a loyal customer and decides to waive the fee this one time. The customer is happy and uses this as a learning experience.

Be Ready to Play Hardball

Do not cave automatically when your bank refuses your request. You need to be persistent and play hardball. Let them know you are not going down without a fight. Keep it civil but remain firm. Always remember that you are the customer and can take your business elsewhere. If the first person you talk to does not try to appease you, then go up the chain and speak to a manager or supervisor.

It may sound petty to negotiate over minor fees; however, these small expenses can turn out to be huge when added all up. This is especially true if you have multiple accounts. Hidden fees can creep up on you and steal your hard-earned money. Do not allow them to do so.

Take Advice from the Right People

Be careful who you take advice from, especially when it comes to finances. Many people will turn to family or friends when they need counsel, but this can be detrimental to your results. While those close to you might have your best interest at heart, they will likely give you advice based on emotions, assumptions, and past experience, instead of hard facts. You need to take advice from the right people. In terms of money, this needs to come from a financial expert. You can talk to one personally or utilize many online learning tools.

Before seeking out a financial expert, do your research and make sure the individual is reliable. Look at past reviews of the expert and see what others have been saying about them. Be careful who you give access to in regard to financial matters.

Simple Ways to Keep More of Your Money

I will end this chapter by going over some simple strategies that can effectively help you start saving money overnight. We are all manipulated and tricked in so many ways to give away our money unnecessarily. Spend less money on what you don't want, so you have more to spend on what you do want. Not all of the following tips may apply to you, but whatever advice I can give, I am happy to do so.

Turn off the Television

That's right. Watching less TV can help you hang onto more of your money. There are so many enticing ads that induce people to spend money. While I want you to spend money on things you want, impulse-buying is not the way to go. You may see something on TV that looks exciting, but then have to desire or use for it when it actually arrives. Television can also be a distraction for you, and you can use this time to build your empire, instead.

Practice the 30-Day Rule

This is when you delay instant gratification by waiting 30 days before you purchase something. Chances are, if you still want something after 30 days, then you really want it. If not, it was something that created temporary joy, but no long-term happiness. Taking the time to wait can give you some perspective on whether an item is truly worth it.

Don't Spend Money on things You can do for Free

Once again, I want you to spend money on things you enjoy, but if you can get the same emotions by doing something similar for free, then why wouldn't you. For example, if you love to work out and go to the gym, perhaps you can for a run or exercise at home. If it gives you the same rush, then go for it. If you prefer going to the gym, then keep doing so.

Have a Garage Sale

Go through your closets, drawers, basement, or wherever you stash personal items and try to find things you don't want or need anymore. After this, hold a garage sale or sell things through an online platform of some sort. Get rid of these unwanted items, make some extra cash, and then do what you please with your money.

Eliminate Waste

Wasteful expenses can add up, so eliminate them the best you can. Finish all the food that you buy, turn off the lights when you leave a room, and do not use more water than you have to. These small changes can save you a few bucks here or there, which will ultimately add up.

Buy Quality Appliances that will Last

This goes back to not being a cheapskate. Why would you buy something for cheap, only to have it break down and become useless quickly? Paying $200 for an old fridge and then needing to buy a new one after a couple of months is not very economical and just a waste of time. Instead, buy more expensive appliances the first time and watch them last for years. Many appliance stores offer interest-free payment plans, so you don't have to pay a lump sum all at once.

Cancel Magazine Subscriptions

Honestly, why do you need magazines these days? You can get the same information online. If you absolutely need a magazine for some reason, then buy one from the store, rather than spending money every month on a subscription.

Keep a Notebook for Ideas

We often come up with great money-making ideas on the fly but forget what they are after a day or two. Keep a notebook handy, and anytime you have an idea for making some extra cash, write it down and revisit it later.

Invest in Education

I am not talking about a university here. Of course, that is an option too. I am talking about learning programs, both online and in-person, that can educate you on many topics. Many community programs and centers even offer skills training that you can use later on for extra income. Look at sites like Udemy, which offers great classes online on a wealth of topics. These include subjects related to finance.

Buy Items in Bulk

Determine what items you often use, like paper, staples, pens, paper towels, or any other products, and try to buy them in bulk. Nonperishable items like these will last you a long time. If you plan on buying food in bulk, consider investing in a deep freezer or storage.

Find Out the Benefits Your Company Offers

There are some companies that are quite generous, but their employees don't realize it. Find out the benefits that your company offers and take advantage of them. For example, you could get discounts on car insurance or your phone bill, win tickets to a ball game, receive discounts at certain restaurants, and receive various other freebies.

Eat a Good Breakfast in the Morning

Getting good nutrition in the morning will give you more energy to seize the day. You will also avoid impulsive eating practices because you will not be so hungry all the time. I am talking about a nutrient-dense breakfast here, and not just some toaster pastries or a cup of coffee.

Don't Beat Yourself up over Mistakes

We all make mistakes at some point. It is in your best interest to not dwell on them. It will just be a waste of time and energy. Instead, learn from your mistakes and then move on.

I hope you enjoyed this chapter on how you can keep more of your money and grow it, as well. In the next chapter, I will go over some ways to start increasing your income. Saving strategies can only take you so far. At some point, you need to earn more.

Chapter 4

Saving Money, Spending Money

A young man with a modest salary drove into his neighborhood one day in a new car. This would not be unusual in most cases. People buy new cars all the time. However, on this occasion, the young man had an expensive-looking sports car. His neighbors were quite shocked because this gentleman was not known to be rich. He lived a pretty modest life and did not have a high wage job.

When one of the neighbors congratulated him on the new purchase, the young man turned around and said, "Yeah, it was a steal at the police auction." The neighbor was stunned by where the purchase was made. Inside the car were also some nice historical paintings and appliances, all of which looked to be in mint condition.

The point of this story is that you do not have to go into bankruptcy to be able to live a luxurious life. It pains me to see so many people missing out on what life has to offer because they think they had to hoard all their money for something that might happen in the future. I've got news for you. Money is meant to be enjoyed because you work hard for it. It is your money, and it is meant to be spent.

The focus of this chapter will be on how to spend money on things you enjoy while also having some to save and invest. I am in no way saying that you should go out and buy a million-dollar home when you only make $30,000 per year. However, I also don't want you to go through life, never getting to enjoy what the world has to offer. There is great food, destinations, material objects, and whatever else you may fancy that is ripe for the taking. You deserve to enjoy these things when you are using your own money. I will show you how.

Before we go into these strategies, I want you to follow the pay yourself first (PYF) model. This is a very simple method. Whatever income you bring in, pay yourself first with it before spending it on anything else. For example, if you bring in $1,000 per week, take out 10% of that immediately for savings and investments. You can pay yourself a higher percentage if you choose. After paying yourself, then you can spend your money on whatever else you want or need. If you have money left over after this, then you can choose to put this into your savings or investments too.

Tips for Living Luxuriously

Imagine staying at a beautiful hotel with a beach view, a balcony, gourmet breakfast, and an expensive rental car. Now, imagine only paying about $30 for everything. This would be an amazing deal, right. You are living like a wealthy person, whether you are one or not. Enjoying the finer things in life does not have to ruin you financially. You don't have to choose between paying your bills and enjoying something you love to do. You can have both and still have money for your savings account in the end.

I can't guarantee the life you will end up living, but if you're willing to do some research, you can live a fun life with many adventures while buying many of the items you love. The following are some simple tips to start living luxuriously.

Attending the Symphony for Free

All rich people love the symphony, don't they? Well, that may be quite an assumption; however, going to a concert of this kind is not known to be an inexpensive outing. Of course, you may not have to pay at all. Many of the major symphonies around the country offer free nights for the public. If you are a fan of this type of art, then you can enjoy it without having to pay for it. Just google "Free symphonies" in your area and see what is available.

You can find other concerts in this fashion too. Many well-known bands will put on free concerts, especially if they are from a certain area. If not for free, then at extremely discounted rates. You might be able to see your favorite band or musical group and have decent seats.

Go on a Cruise for Cheap

This is a greater advantage for people who live near cruise ship ports. There are many discount coupons out there for dinner cruises, day cruises, and even long-term cruises. You can go on a number of these for a fraction of the cost. There are many websites to find cruises to far-off destinations, like the Caribbean, Bahamas, Alaska, and even Europe, for very affordable prices. Once you are on the ship, many of the buffets and food items are paid for. Of course, you will still need to pay extra for unlimited dining and at certain restaurants, as well.

Fodor.com is a website that gives guidance on finding cheap cruises. Individuals have found cruises to places like the Bahamas for less than $200, which is a steal. Once again, figure out how much of the food and excursions will be included in this price tag. If you are not interested in long cruises to far-off destinations, then you can go on multiple day cruises and still spend less than $50, while still getting most of the amenities. With these types of deals, you can truly live like a rich person without breaking the bank.

This tip may sound useless to those who don't live near cruise terminals but check out what your particular area offers. They don't just do cruises on the ocean. Several lakes and rivers, etc., offer them, as well. Don't just take a price that is given to you at face value, either. Look at various resources and determine what your best options are.

Stay in Luxury Hotels, Without Luxurious Prices

Points from credit cards and hotel membership cards can add up quickly by doing regular, everyday things, like buying groceries or pumping gas. In addition, hotel cards will earn you points as you stay at their hotels and end up getting free or discounted nights. Some amazing hotel chains you could end up staying at are the Hyatt and Marriot.

Buy Quality Used Art

What do you often see when you go into rich People's homes? A lot of paintings and artifacts that really serve no purpose besides being decorative. Of course, you have no idea how much these paintings actually are or if the people went into debt to look good. You can decorate your own space with these types of art by buying them at discounted prices. Try rummaging through garage sales, flea markets, and thrift stores. You will not believe some of the fine items you will find at these locations.

Sellers have been known to give away autographed items of legendary sports stars or paintings from well-known artists at a steal of a price, whether knowingly or unknowingly. Imagine finding a Picasso painting worth thousands of dollars for just a fistful of cash at a thrift store. This might sound far-fetched, but it has happened before. You might as well take your chances.

Many individuals make a business out of finding quality items at a discounted rate and selling them for large profits. This is something you should consider down the line to make some extra money. It may even lead you to become rich.

Buy a Luxury Car

Have you always wanted a luxury car of some sort? Does a Cadillac, Mercedes-Benz, or other high-quality car sound good to you? Well, you can start driving one today and get it for a fairly good deal. The only catch is that someone has owned the car before. Yes, I am talking about used luxury cars here. Many people get twisted up when they hear the words "used car," but any car that has been driven off the lot by its owner for just a few miles is pre-owned and used. Cars drop in value immediately and continue to do so over the years. If you can buy a slightly used car with just a couple of thousand miles on it for thousands of dollars less, then why not do so?

Even luxury cars drop in value quickly. It is estimated that a 10-year old car can be purchased for 1/10 of its original value. If you don't want a car this old, then one that's just a couple of years, or even a few months, old can be yours at a severely discounted rate. Imagine driving down the road in luxury without having to pay for luxury.

Not Just Cars, but Other Luxury Items

Pre-owned items at a discounted rate are not just exclusive to cars. You can buy many luxury items that are used but still in great condition. For example, you can find a designer handbag worth thousands of dollars for less than $100. I am not talking about knock-off brands here, but actual designer products. There are also sites, like vincerowatches.com, where you can buy some amazing wristwatches for a fraction of the price. The goal here is not to look rich for others but feel rich yourself and start feeling good. You can also find great items on auction sites, like eBay, and even Amazon offers great deals. Here's a trick: If you see an item at a store that you like, quickly research it on amazon to see if you can save and how much.

Find a Cheap Home in an Expensive City

Many homebuyers avoid cities or towns that they love because the cost of living there is ridiculous. Even with higher wages, it doesn't account for how much you'll be spending on a home and other necessities. However, you can actually find affordable homes in expensive cities, if you know how to look. You must keep an open mind when looking for certain types of homes. For example, in a city like Naples, Florida, where home prices can be in the millions, you can find condos for less than $100,000. My point here is that you shouldn't dismiss the idea of living in an expensive city filled with millionaires at first glance. If you are willing to look deeper, you can find some great deals.

On the flip side of this, if you do not really care what town you live in, then you can find amazing homes that look like mansions in certain areas. For example, a 3,000 square-foot home would cost an arm and a leg in San Francisco or New York City; you can find them for 1/3 the price in places like Dallas or Oklahoma City. Bear in mind, living in a city with rich people can bring you a lot of advantages. For example, the worth on your home can go up tremendously down the line, plus there are several amenities, like free parking at beaches, free concerts, and free access to many clubs and organizations.

There is a saying out there that you become who you spend the most amount of time with. If you are surrounded by millionaires, you are bound to become one yourself, if you're willing to do what it takes.

Expensive Restaurants? Not Really

Are there specific types of food you want to try or restaurants you want to visit, but are horrified of getting the bill afterward? Well, I can say that the ambiance in an expensive restaurant is what makes it worth it. So, if there is a place you want to try, go there and just order an appetizer or dessert. Even at expensive restaurants, these selections will not break the bank for you. From here, just enjoy the atmosphere of the place and take it all in. If the restaurant has a patio, then try to get a patio seat.

There is a much deeper meaning to all of these tips. Once you get a taste of what it's like to be rich, you will be motivated to grow your wealth. Having the finer things in life, like luxury items, great travel experiences, wining, and dining at the finest restaurants, and staying at immaculate hotels is addicting. To fuel this addiction, you will continue to look for deals and even ways to grow your riches.

Why Happiness Should be the End Goal

After everything is said and done, your ultimate goal should not be the millions of dollars, but the happiness that comes from the lifestyle it creates. Why should you not enjoy something in life because it is too expensive or out of your reach? The answer is that you should not have to. If you want to live your life in a certain manner, then figure out how to do so. Do not just stand on the sidelines and watch life pass you by.

The funny thing is, even though happiness should be the most important goal someone seeks out, very few people actually ask about it. They ask about your career if you have a family, where you live, and what your goals are. They never ask, "Are you happy?" People will simply assume you are or aren't based on what their perceived image of happiness is. I want all of you to imagine the perfect life that will make you feel nothing but positive. This will mean something different for every person. In the end, it is the life you should work towards.

So, if you have been limiting yourself because you can't afford things or don't have the resources, then it's time to get out of this funk. When you limit yourself, you are essentially saying that you are not worthy of happiness. This is a false way of thinking because everyone can achieve this state of mind, and they have the right to do so. With all of the tips I went over earlier in this chapter, the underlying theme is that you should figure out how to live the life you want and never use the excuse of not being able to afford it.

"The most important thing is to enjoy your life-to be happy-It's all that matters."
-Aubrey Hepburn

Hanging Out With Millionaires

You need to choose your friends wisely. You need to hang around people who are living the type of life you want so that you can be inspired and pick up on their habits. Sorry to say, but if you spend all of your time with someone who just barely gets by in life, is not ambitious, and is more interested in binge-watching a bunch of Netflix series than building an empire, you will also fall into this boat. However, if you hang around someone who is inspired, works hard, is constantly learning, and busy building an empire, then you will work to improve yourself in this manner.

I am not trying to insult anyone's lifestyle. However, if you want to become a millionaire, then you must start acting like one. The best way to learn is to spend time with them. I am not saying you should act like you're better than people. I am just stating the fact that financially wealthy people look at the world differently, especially in regard to how they spend their time. Millionaires do not waste time because they see it as their greatest asset. It is something they will never get back, so they embrace it every moment of their lives. The worst thing you can do to a millionaire is to waste their time. They will resent you heavily for it.

A major factor for the financially wealthy is the ability to network with other rich people. If you start hanging out where the millionaires do, you will meet and get to know many of them. You might even develop some relationships. Without sounding too pushy, ask these individuals where they can go to learn about their work and what they do. Ask if you can take them out for lunch sometime. Show a genuine interest in someone can make them feel appreciated. The worst thing that can happen when you ask is that they say no. However, in a room full of rich people, you are bound to learn something, as long as you remain persistent.

I urge you to take a look at your inner circle to see what path you are headed down. Again, this is not meant to be insulting, but we all choose our own pathways, and to become the millionaire you want to be, you must pick your friends wisely.

Chapter 5

Managing Your Time and Finances

What do you think Mark Wahlberg, Oprah Winfrey, or Dwayne "The Rock" Johnson did today? While I did not follow them around, I reckon they spend their time building their empire, improving their health, and spending time with their family. They probably did not work on balancing their checkbooks or walking into a bank to make a deposit. Why is that? Because they either hire individuals to take care of their financial matters for them or have everything automated. They do not have time to focus on mundane work like this.

You need to begin acting in the same fashion. There is a technique that many life coaches use that is called the "Eisenhower Matrix." This method is used to determine what areas of your life need the most attention, what can be delegated, and what can be cast aside completely because it brings you no value. The sections of the matrix are as follows:

- Important and urgent tasks that need to be done well and ASAP. These are the things that require most of your attention.
- Important but not urgent tasks need to be completed by you but don't have a deadline coming up soon.
- Not important, but urgent tasks are those that need to be done quickly but do not require a lot of your attention. These are tasks that can be delegated. This section is where your trips to the

bank and taking care of unimportant financial matters, like money transfers, can fall into.
- The last section is unimportant and non-urgent tasks that don't need to be done at all, like surfing social media.

I advise that if you are still using the old school methods of walking into a bank, or doing transfers manually, that you hire a trusted assistant to do it for you. Anything that does not require your presence should be delegated. This will save you time so you can focus your attention on more important matters.

Mark Wahlberg is not worried about going to the bank to make a deposit. He is spending time reading scripts, talking to his agent, going over contracts, and working out. He delegates whatever he can get away with, and you must start doing the same thing if you want to maximize your potential.

Knowing When to Delegate

To become a millionaire, you cannot spend much of your time on tasks that you don't need to do. Think about how much time is wasted standing in line or waiting on hold during a phone call. At some point, you must delegate things to other people. Your professional life will be much different when you only focus on high-level tasks that require your full attention. Whatever responsibilities that don't need your full attention should be handed over to someone else. Assess your duties and determine what items you don't need to touch. These are often mundane tasks that anyone can do, like rescheduling appointments, making phone calls, sending emails, or organizing the office. If you can avoid these things that keep you away from more critical work, then start delegating them as soon as you can.

Also, you can delegate work that other people can do better than you. This holds true for both your personal and professional life. For example, you can delegate projects at your home that you are not an expert at by hiring someone to do them. These can include things like landscaping, building a deck, or various construction projects inside the home. If you don't know how to do these things, then it will not be worth your time to learn them. Instead, hire a trusted expert to do these things for you and focus on other areas of your life. In addition, work-related tasks, like developing a website or copywriting, require a certain level of skill. There are experts who can perform these projects for you. You may not think a website developer is a good investment, but once you start getting more business because of a professionally crafted website, you will thank that developer incessantly.

"Surround yourself with the best people you can find, delegate authority, and don't interfere as long as the policy you've decided upon is being carried out."

A major reason people refuse to delegate is because of fear. They are afraid that another person cannot do the tasks as needed, even when they are low-level. Another reason is resistance to spending extra money to hire someone and then have to train them to perform the tasks adequately. For this, you must determine what the value of your time is compared to how much you will pay someone to take work off your plate. There will certainly be a training period when you first bring someone on to help you, but once they are up and running, you will save a lot of time. My advice here is to give people a chance to learn, but if they are not motivated or making progress, then it is time to move on. Never allow someone to waste too much of your time.

Another issue here is the fear of taking responsibility. If you delegate a task to someone, you are still ultimately responsible for how things turn out. Many people have a hard time accepting this fact and decide to do everything themselves, or micromanage anything they delegate, which defeats the purpose of saving time. All I can say is that before you assign a project to someone, make sure they have the ability to do it. The first tasks you want to assign are the lowest level ones that require no training and little supervision. From there, hire based on qualifications and get adequate references.

I hope you see the value in delegation because it will make you so much more productive. Millionaires get things done, and one of the reasons is that they don't do everything themselves. Anyone at the top tier of any industry has great people working for them. If you are ready to start delegating and removing items from your plate, then start using these action steps to make the most effective use of your time.

- Carefully map out exactly what you need to be done. You must have clear expectations that cannot keep changing.
- Once you fully understand what needs to get done, then it's time to convey this information to the person you are delegating to. Be sure everything is clear on timing, deadlines, context, and follow-up.

- After going over everything, confirm understanding. Never assume that a person understands what you told them. Ask questions along the way and have them repeat back to what you told them. They don't have to regurgitate verbatim what you told them, but just provide a summary to ensure understanding.
- Confirm commitment of the tasks. Make sure the individual is willing and ready to take it on. This is a critical step that is missed because people assume others have accepted a task when they actually haven't. Direct and clear communication is needed here.
- Avoid "reverse delegation." This is when delegated tasks get returned back. If you find a person lost and confused about what they took on, then coach them and help them find the necessary resources. Do not absolve them of the responsibility and take a task back. You will have to start from square one if you do.
- Hold accountability over the person you delegate to. Make sure they are giving you updates on what has been done so you can ensure your responsibilities are not falling through the cracks.

The more you delegate, the easier it will become. Just like anything else, it takes practice. Start today and determine what simple duties you can start handing over to other people. You will be amazed at how much of your day open up once you find the right people to help you get things done.

Delegating Finances

Tasks related to finances fall under both busywork and complicated information. Basically, there are certain undertakings that are just mundane and a waste of time. These can include making deposits, sending emails, being on hold over the phone, paying bills, and making transfers. Honestly, you do not have to perform these duties as you can hire an assistant to do them for you. It doesn't take a genius to make a deposit at a bank or pay bills over the phone as long as they have the right information. Other functions might be too complicated for a layperson to understand, and this is where an expert in finances comes into play. Many times, more complicated issues are related to investing.

Investing can seem like a rollercoaster with all of the ups and downs that occur in the market. Also, different experts will have their own varying opinions on what will work and what won't. It can be hard to tell when and if the stock market will crash, and this can bring out many different feelings in a person. When you bring emotions into your finances, that is when poor decisions are made. It may benefit you to hire a trusted financial expert to make investment decisions for you on a daily basis. Your role will simply be to make sure they are doing their job. The financial expert should always explain to you why you are either gaining or losing money on your investments and what future projections are expected to be.

As your income goes up, your finances will become more complex. You might start dealing with many different accounts, and some solid financial decisions will need to be made. A good financial planner can help you with this complexity. Some important questions they can answer for you include: How to minimize taxes legally? How to invest your money? Which retirement accounts should you contribute to? How long can you live off your current savings and investments? Is your money well-protected? How many liabilities vs. assets do you own? At the very least, a personal financial advisor can help you make critical decisions based on their knowledge and experience. You won't have to worry about daily market performances without their guidance.

Finally, you do not have to spend an exorbitant amount of time following the market. Unless you are a professional stockbroker or investor, this will not be worth your time. Instead, hire an expert who can keep track of the market for you. A good financial planner or advisor can build a balanced portfolio for you and then help it grow through various strategies that balance risks and rewards. You will also get access to the information you would not have time to find on your own.

If you were to have medical issues, you would seek out a doctor. If you have legal problems, then you would seek out an attorney. If you want to build a house, then you would hire a contractor. Therefore, why would you not hire a financial planner to deal with your complicated money matters? Even if you understand finances and investments, if it is not your fulltime occupation, you are better off hiring an expert and then following up with them regularly. You do not have to go at it alone when it comes to handling your wealth. In fact, most millionaires understand this is the best route for them to take.

How to Automate Finances

With the advanced technology and ability to do things electronically, automating finances has never been easier and more appropriate. You can easily transfer between accounts without having to do anything. After the initial setup, everything moves around automatically, and the only time you need to intervene is when you need to make changes. It is almost unnecessary to walk into a bank or financial institution these days. Of course, having that option is still nice, but if you can avoid it and still have the same, or better results, then automation is the way to go.

The focus of this section will be how to automate all of your finances in an efficient, responsible, and safe manner. Your money will move around like magic with little intervention from you. Your sole responsibility is to make sure everything is moving around smoothly without hiccups. The following are some specific action steps to start you on your automation journey.

Open the Appropriate Accounts

The first thing you need to do is open the right accounts to get the process started. Your primary checking account will serve as the central location for money coming in and going out. Basically, you will have cash flow coming in at predetermined times, which can be from paychecks, business income, royalties, investment dividends, alimony, or various other sources. Always have an idea of when money will be flowing into this account and always keep a cash cushion to prevent an overdraw. Determine what the minimum amount you always want in this account and never let it fall below that. Most people keep about 25-30% of their monthly income as their minimum.

Pay Yourself First

I have discussed the "pay yourself first" philosophy, and it is very important if you want to maintain the automation process. First, you need to pay yourself first to create the cash cushion you need in step one. After you create this cushion, continue to set aside a certain percentage of your income every time it comes in to stay in your account. As soon as your income hits your account, have a portion of this redirected immediately to an emergency, savings, and retirement, accounts. Literally, before paying any bills, buying groceries, paying down loans, or getting gifts, pay yourself first. People who do not follow the pay yourself first philosophy generally spend everything they make, or even more than they make.

Set Up Automatic Payments

Never worry about forgetting what your bill due date is. Don't spend your day sifting through bills and paying manually. This is just a waste of time that you can use towards something else. Automate all of your bills that can be automated, which should be most, if not all, of them. As long as you make sure you maintain your minimum cash cushion, this process should go seamlessly. This will eliminate worry about whether bills are being paid or not.

Automate Contributions to Investment Accounts

After your savings and bills are being taken care of automatically, the next step is to set up for your investment accounts. Determine a specific time each month where a certain amount of your finances from your checking account will transfer to all of your investment accounts. If you do not want everything to be shifted at the same time, then you can set it up for half to be transferred at the beginning of the month, and the other half in the middle. For example, you can transfer $500 at the beginning of the month to your mutual fund and index fund, while transferring another $500 in the middle of the month to your other brokerage accounts. These numbers are just examples.

If your company offers their own retirement accounts, like a 401(k) or 403(b), then you can certainly contribute to those, as well. Contribute enough to match your employer's contributions.

Increase Your Automated Transfers Over Time

My hope is that you will work on increasing your income, which means you should be transferring more of this income to your savings and investment accounts. You will also need to keep a higher minimum cash cushion in your checking account. Many online investment platforms and online banks will allow you to increase your recurring contributions on a yearly basis. You can also set up automatic escalation. The benefit here is that it allows you to maintain a proper spend/save ratio as your salary increases.

Overall, automation will allow you to remain disciplined with your money while having a certain amount to use for spending. If you couple automation with many of the other techniques I have gone over in previous chapters, then you will have good control of your finances, which is essential to growing your wealth and becoming a millionaire.

Chapter 6

Managing Major Expenses Stress-Free

There is no way around it. You will be hit with major expenses throughout your life. Some of these are planned, like mortgage or rent, while others are unexpected, like medical emergencies or car problems. In many cases, the stress that comes from these expenses are overwhelming, which can cause most people to not think straight. No one wants to be homeless or lose everything they worked for, which is often the biggest fear that comes with major expenses.

While stress is a human emotion that can be nearly impossible to get rid of, the focus of this chapter will be how to manage your stress and not be overtaken by it. As various expenses come your way, keeping a level head is essential in making rational decisions. Stress can lead to emotionally based decisions, which may result in poor financial choices. When it comes to money, you want to avoid decisions made on impulse. For example, don't automatically pull money from your savings and investment accounts to use on emergencies when there is the first sign of trouble.

One of the main reasons millionaires reach the level they are at is because they know how to manage stress and don't let it control them. Instead, they use it to motivate them. As you increase your wealth, your expenses will also rise, and you must learn to keep a calm head about yourself.

Unfortunately, stress over money does not only affect your finances. It can also impact your health. Ongoing stress can lead to an increased risk of heart disease, diabetes, sleep problems, and even certain cancers. Not only that, but it can also lead to unhealthy behaviors, like overeating and alcohol use. It is important to not let your stress get out of hand; otherwise, your life will suffer in immense ways. Let's go over some ways to tackle stress while managing your major expenses.

How to Cope with Financial Stress

Once you learn how to cope with financial stress, you will effectively be able to manage your money situation. You will have more control in your life, as a result, and won't become overwhelmed with the major expenses that occur in your life. The following are some tips to help you start dealing with financial stress.

- Understand the debt cycle, which is continual borrowing that leads to increased debt. While some debt can be good, like the kind that gives you a return, at some point, the debt needs to be paid off. You have to begin controlling how much you borrow before you get too down under. Once you understand the debt cycle, then you can work your way out of debt and start building towards your future.
- Declutter your money and budget. Life is constantly changing, and you may start increasing your income or spending without realizing what's going on. This is especially true when you start using automation, as I described in the previous chapter. Set aside some time once a month to organize and declutter the money coming in and going out. You will have more control over your money and feel less stressed.

- Work on ways to increase your income. I will get into this more during the next chapter, but increasing your income and managing it properly will reduce your stress about your expenses.
- Focus on general stress management techniques. There are many ways you can reduce your stress level as a whole.
  - Keep a positive attitude.
  - Accept that there are things you cannot control
  - Exercise regularly
  - Practice mindfulness through things like yoga
  - Make time to things that you love
  - Spend time with those you genuinely enjoy being around
  - Learn to manage your time more effectively.

Many of the general stress management techniques will help you remain focused in regard to finances.

Managing Unexpected Expenses

Unexpected expenses are one of the most common ways that people become stressed about their finances. Even if the expense is not that much, the fact that it came out of nowhere can still hurt. The funny thing is, a person won't care much about spending $200 on a gift for themselves, but $200 on emergencies can harm their psyche. However, unexpected expenses do not have to tear you down, and they won't if you don't let them. In this section, I will go over some of the most common unexpected expenses and how you can manage them with as little stress as possible.

Medical Emergencies

Certain healthcare costs, like medications and checkups, are usually expected expenses, and you can plan ahead of time on how to pay for them. Even routine procedures, like a root canal, nonemergency surgery, or a Lasik procedure, can be saved up for. However, when you have a medical emergency, there is no plan for that. It happens out of nowhere, and you cannot predict this expense. The best you can do is prepare for it ahead of time. A visit to the emergency room alone can cost thousands of dollars, and that is without any major tests or procedures that may need to be done.

Dealing with a medical emergency is difficult enough without the financial burdens on top of it. In fact, finances generally cause more stress than the emergency itself. Of course, the simplest way to avoid this type of expense is to never get sick, which is not practical advice at all. Even if you don't become ill, you never know when a major injury will occur.

You can certainly make simple choices to improve your health, like a healthy diet, regular exercise, and going in for regular checkups to detect problems before they become too big. In addition, you can create more safety in your life by avoiding too many dangerous situations. Once again, none of this is a guarantee. Medical emergencies do not have to discriminate, and any one of us can become stuck in this situation.

I spoke in an earlier chapter about healthcare, which is definitely a necessity. If you don't want to pay for total health coverage and your employer doesn't off it, then you can choose a "catastrophic" health plan. These don't cover basic care but can protect you against the kind of emergencies that will bankrupt you. You can get these kinds of plans for lower than $200 per month. These plans usually have high deductibles, so keep that in mind too. To supplement "catastrophic" health insurance, I recommend setting up a flexible spending account. This is where your pretax dollars from your income transfer to and you can use it to pay for deductibles, medications, and other healthcare bills. A flexible spending account can provide you extra cushioning so you can avoid dipping into your savings or emergency funds to pay for unexpected medical expenses.

There are other ways you can receive healthcare but cut healthcare costs. For example, you may not need to go to an emergency room for every medical issue. If it's not a true emergency and you are just feeling sick, try to get into your doctor's office. If you can't wait for the appointment, then consider a walk-in clinic or urgent care. In addition, you can opt for cheaper treatments, like generic medications, or find out ways to reduce the need for prescriptions by making lifestyle changes. For example, if you lose a significant amount of weight, then it might lower your blood pressure naturally. Of course, I am not here to give medical advice.

Finally, if all else fails and you get stuck with a major medical bill, then don't stress. Talk to the hospital about reducing your payments. Many hospitals are happy to work with individuals to create reasonable financing options. They would rather do this than have someone not pay at all.

Pet Emergencies

We love our furry friends and want to do what is best for them. This included taking care of them when they get sick or injured. Having to rush a family pet to the emergency vet can be like having to take a family member to the hospital. What's worse is when you get the bill for treatment. While pet emergencies are not as financially draining as emergencies for people, they can still set you back a pretty penny.

After the issue is taken care of, you could end up owing thousands of dollars in medical bills. Unfortunately, you cannot protect your pet from everything and could end up dealing with a major expense. To avoid these, many people buy pet insurance, which will cover the cost of most medical bills. However, this type of insurance can have many restrictions, so a better option for you might be to set up an emergency account solely for expenses related to your pet.

If all else fails and you get stuck with a major medical bill anyway, then you can discuss with your vet a plan to help pay off your debt. At the very least, you can work out a payment plan to help avoid paying off a large bill all at once. There are also various charities and animal welfare groups who are ready to help needy pet owners with their vet bills. The humane society website is a great resource to find this type of health. To avoid major expenses in the future, you can seek out cheaper providers. For example, veterinary schools and animal shelters run low-cost clinics for owners who need it.

If you decide to own a pet someday, then I advise you to always be prepared for unexpected expenses. The animal is relying on you for care and protection, so being able to provide health and emergency care is essential. Until you have the ability to do this, I would avoid getting a pet altogether.

Major Auto Repairs

If you own a car, then you must spend a good amount of money each year to keep it running smoothly. While you can predict certain maintenance costs, like new tires, timing belts, or regular oil changes, other repairs are not so easy to predict. The best way to avoid expensive repairs is to make sure your car service is always up-to-date and gets regularly scheduled maintenance. By doing this, many issues can be detected early and be taken care of before there is a major issue down the line.

Still, unexpected repair costs can occur, and this can cost you thousands of dollars. Of course, auto insurance can deal with repairs related to an accident, after you pay for the deductible. But what about other types of repairs, especially those related to wear and tear.

One of the major ways to delay repair costs is to drive as little as possible. Whenever you can walk, ride a bike, or take public transport. If you live in a major city with great public transport, then you may not even need a car. If you are a handy person and enjoy working on cars, then you can even do some simple repairs yourself.

You can always buy a manufacturer's warranty, or for an older vehicle, mechanical breakdown insurance. However, the premiums and annual costs you end up paying may not be worth it. Instead, a better option for you is to have an emergency fund set up specifically for car repairs. Also, you can just have a general emergency fund to avoid too many accounts to manage.

To prevent excessive bills in the future, make sure you have a roadside service plan to help with things like towing, jumpstarts, and being stranded on the side of the road. Triple-A is the most classic example of this, but many of the major insurance companies are offering plans like this now. In summary, the best way to deal with major care repairs is to avoid them as much as you can.

Major Home Repairs

Having your own home is bound to cost you a certain amount in repairs every year. It is impossible to know how much because items can always break unexpectedly. If you are not ready for these types of expenses, then I recommend that you keep renting. Renting can have its own benefits, one of them being not worrying about repair costs.

You can help to avoid major home repairs by keeping up-to-date on general maintenance. For example, have your air conditioner checked every year, perform regular maintenance on your water heater, and make sure you are doing things like winterizing your sprinklers. Take care of smaller problems when you find them; otherwise, they will turn into major problems.

If you are able to do maintenance work yourself, then do so. If not, then hire a good contractor. You can search for trustworthy personnel on sites like Angie's List or Home Advisor. If possible, always get a free quote first from multiple individuals or companies and find out if there are payment plans for larger projects.

Homeowners insurance will cover the cost of many repairs, but not all of them. Much of this will depend on the policy you own. You can also buy a home warranty that covers many large repair costs. All you have to do is pay the repair person a small deductible, and then the warranty company will cover the rest. American Home Shields is an example of a home warranty company. If your dishwasher, water heater, or air conditioner breaks down, then contact your home warranty company, and they can look for covered contractors.

Just like with all the other unexpected expenses, do whatever you can to build up an emergency account. This account should be your go-to for unexpected repairs before you even think about dipping into your checking or savings funds.

These are just some of the unexpected repairs that can come up. The best way to manage all of them is to be as prepared as you can. After that, don't overly stress about them. Take care of what you can control and then manage the rest of the issues as they come up.

Paying Your Mortgage Quicker

A great way to reduce mortgage stress is to find ways to pay it off sooner. When you do this, not only will you own your home outright much more quickly, but you will actually end up paying a lot less. This is mainly due to paying less in interest payments. There are several tricks you can use to make this happen, especially if you have extra cash lying around. Imagine not having a monthly mortgage payment because you paid it off in half the time. This will open up your finances for other things you would rather buy. Also, you will be able to put more towards your savings and investments.

Make Extra Payments

You can always contribute more than your monthly mortgage payment. If you can, apply a little extra towards your principal every month. Even an extra $100-$200 a month more can go a long way. Paying an extra $200, for example, will put an additional $2,400 a month towards your balance. In 10 years, you will have put an additional $24,000. That's quite a bit extra to help bring down your overall balance.

Another way to make extra payments is to split your mortgage. So, instead of paying monthly, you will pay biweekly. The Biweekly payments will end up being slightly more together than the individual monthly payment, but not really enough to put a dent in most budgets. With the extra payment amount being put in each month, it will turn out to be the equivalent of 13 monthly payments instead of 12. This could mean paying off your mortgage a few years early. In addition, you will have more in your equity if you decide to sell the home.

Refinance Your Mortgage

Refinancing only makes sense if you will be able to get a lower interest rate. Therefore, do your research on current interest rates and talk to your lender to about how much lower you can get yours. Be aware of the fees that come with refinancing and make sure they do not offset the savings you will receive.

You can also refinance from a 30-year to a 15-year loan, which will give you lower interest rates and allow you to pay off your mortgage sooner. You can use a mortgage calculator to determine what your new monthly payment amount will be. If you can afford it, then why not try to pay off your mortgage quicker.

Recast Your Mortgage

Recasting differs refinancing since your existing loan does not change. With this process, a lump sum is paid towards the principal. The lender will then readjust your payment length schedule. The loan term will be shorter, as a result.

With recasting, the fees are significantly lower than with refinancing, which is a huge benefit in this regard; a few hundred dollars compared to a few thousand. If your interest rate is good and you're happy with it, then you get to keep it. If your interest rate is high, though, then refinancing might be a better option.

Never feel bad about putting more money towards your mortgage principal balance. You are essentially putting money back in your own pocket. When you are well ahead of schedule in paying off your mortgage loan, it can significantly reduce your stress levels. If you own a mortgage, it needs to be paid off, so always figure out a way to do so. You don't want to get behind on these because the lenders will notice, and your chances of getting assistance will go down. If you feel like you need help, ask for it because major problems ensue.

Minor Expenses You Should Not Worry About

Sometimes, people become stressed over minor expenses they make every day. The truth is, a pack of gum here, or a cup of coffee there, will probably not break the bank for you, especially if you think about money in the way that's described in this book. A major theme I have tried to promote is the idea of experiences over money. Do the things you enjoy, and don't be overly stressed about the money you are spending. While most financial advisors will tell you to skip that café and make coffee at home, I will tell you to buy that cup of coffee you love drinking.

Remember, money is infinite, and you can always make more. Time and opportunity will not always exist. When you look back at life, you will recall the fun things you did and not how much money you were able to save up. Congratulations! It's the end of your days, and you have millions of dollars that you didn't enjoy and won't get to now. I don't want to turn this book dark, but my point is, don't be so frugal to the extent you don't enjoy your life. Life is meant for experiences and not to dwell on every little problem. I will end this chapter by going over the common small expenses that people become stressed over, that they shouldn't. Spending your money on these items will not be the end of the world.

- Daily coffee: If you enjoy getting a daily cup of coffee from your favorite café, then do so. This can be a relaxing activity and even get the day going for you in the morning.
- Haircuts: Haircuts can make you look and feel like a different person. If you have to shell out a few extra bucks to go to a barber or styling you like, then don't feel guilty about the cost. This is an investment in you. Now, if someone can cut your hair for $20 and do just as good of a job as someone who charges $30, then the choice is

simple. Otherwise, go for the more expensive one.

- Netflix: Netflix is a very cost-effective method of getting entertainment, which we all need in our lives for fun. $10 per month to watch unlimited shows and movies from the comfort of your home is not a bad deal.
- Gym memberships: The gym membership is another investment you make in yourself. As long as you are using it, this monthly expense is worth it to stay healthy. It is another cost-effective way to spend your time. Get the best price on membership that you can, but also make sure the gym is to your liking.
- Healthcare: Yes, it sucks to pay a couple of hundred dollars for checkups, dental visits, medications, and other minor procedures. Do you know what sucks more? Ignoring these expenses and then having bigger problems down the line. A toothache, for instance, can require a minor cleaning when caught early but turn into a root canal or tooth extraction down the line if no interventions are done. Do not ignore your health now because more problems may persist down the line.
- The occasional book or video game purchase: Before anyone starts, yes, people do still buy physical books and video games. If you are one, do not stress over this expense. This is a form of entertainment that you deserve in your life for working hard and being a responsible adult.
- Tax preparation: It can cost extra to hire a professional to do your taxes, but you can save money down the line and avoid major problems with the IRS when you do so.

- Laundry services: While you can do laundry in your home or at the laundromat, there is no denying it is a timewaster. Especially if you have a big family, hiring someone to do your laundry can free you up for more productive activities. It also does not cost that much to have someone do your laundry for you—usually, just a few dollars per round. I am not referring to dry-cleaning here.

The bottom line is, don't stress over money because you will always be able to make more. Worrying about it will not be worth your time, which you can use for something more productive, like making extra money. This will be the topic for the next and final chapter.

Chapter 7
Increase Your Income

There is a reason I chose this as the final chapter. Before you can benefit from making extra income, you need to learn how to manage and think about money in a different way. That was the focus of the previous chapters, which leads us up to this point. I will now go over several ways to increase your income. There are many paths to take, and the one I give you here are just examples. The main idea I want to get across is that money is in abundance, so never feel like you can't get your share of the pie. Stop thinking about cutting your expenses, and start finding ways to increase your income.

How to Increase Your Salary at Work

One of the simplest ways to make more money is to tap into the resource you already have, which is your current employer. While the way to go about this can be individualized based on the management and work environment, the following are a few tips that most people can use.

Know Your Role at Work

To even be considered for a bump in pay, you must be doing well at your job. This is why it's important to know exactly what your role is and follow it. Understand your responsibilities to make sure you are not missing anything. If you haven't already, ask for a meeting with a supervisor and discuss with them what your role and responsibilities are. This way, it will be clear to you, and your higher-ups will appreciate the initiative. As you are gathering this information, determine what the most critical items to focus on are. Of course, these can change on a daily basis.

From here, start doing what is expected of you. If you have unique skills that can make you more productive at your job, then consider using those. Sometimes, just doing what is expected of you is enough to impress the bosses and eventually get a raise. With the work environment that exists within some companies, you might end up being the most productive person there, which is sad when you think about it.

Prepare Yourself

Now that you are clear about what is expected of you, it's time to start preparing for success. Maybe during the meeting with your supervisor, you realized you were falling short in some areas. That's okay because we can start improving on that. Keep a list of tasks that you need to complete every day based on priority. If you need to make a new list every morning, then do so. Stick to this list and don't falter. Avoid going back into your old habits. Whatever work you are doing, no matter how trivial it seems, put your full effort in and focus on the task at hand.

If you are finding yourself completing your projects in record time, then consider taking on more responsibilities. Tell your manager that you can handle some extra work, and if you've done everything else well, then they will be thrilled to have you take on more. You can also learn new skills that will make you more valuable to your company. Touch base with your supervisor to see what areas they need more help in. Always increasing your skillset can help prevent you from getting downsized in the future.

Go the Extra Mile

Always be willing to go the extra mile at work. Once you have your scheduled work done and completed, touch base with your supervisor to see what else you can do. Always asks permission first because you don't want to step on anyone's toes. When you do more than what you're paid for, you will eventually get paid more for what you do.

An employee will tell their boss that if they got paid more, they would do more. However, most bosses will tell their employees that if they do more, they will be paid more. Make your boss happy by doing more. Even if it doesn't bring you a higher salary right away, it will give you good marks for the future. They will not forget your hard work, and when the time for raises and promotions comes around, the opportunities will do to the hardest workers.

Be Likable

You don't have to be friends with everyone while working, but you should be likable and approachable. This is a major factor in increasing your salary and can even carry more weight than your work ethic or productivity. If your bosses like you, they will reward you. That's just the way it is.

You become more likable by maintaining positivity, talking well about others, not complaining incessantly, and spreading joy throughout the office. When someone does something well, no matter how small, praise them for it. Make your coworkers feel special. Also, be trustworthy. When you say you will do something, do it, no matter how minor. When your supervisors feel they can trust you, they are more likely to reward you with a higher salary.

Ask For it

Once you understand your roles and responsibilities, continuously go the extra mile, and built up your trust and reliability, the next step is to go out on a limb and ask for a higher salary. If you think you deserve it, then why not ask for it? When you go into ask, be prepared to let your boss know why without appearing braggadocious. Don't be afraid to ask because the worst thing they can say is no. Of course, if you feel like you deserve a raise, you can always go out and find a new job and use them as a negotiating tactic. Mind you, this can often build resentment, but you need to do what's best for you. Keep it as professional as possible.

When you are ready to make this commitment, use this template:

- Be patients and know the right time to ask for a raise. You cannot expect to get one every time you do something well. Generally, asking for one on an annual basis is a good rule-of-thumb.
- Make a case for why you deserve one. Don't sell yourself short, but don't be braggadocious either. Simply list the accomplishments you have had, the growth you have made as an employee, the positive attributes you bring, and any extra skills you have picked up. For example, did you receive any new certifications that make you more valuable?
- Ask for feedback, and be ready to accept criticism. Nobody is perfect, but this will show

your boss that you are still willing to learn and grow.

- Have a specific number in mind. Don't just ask for a general raise. For example, tell them you deserve $10,000 extra per year. They may negotiate down, but at least you have a good starting point.
- Keep it professional, and don't bring your personal life into it. Instead of discussing your financial problems at home, discuss the progress you have made at work.
- Always thank your boss for their time. Be gracious, whether you get the raise or not. Don't take it personally if you don't. There might be many factors involved which can prevent you from getting a raise at the moment. Don't give up and try again after a few months.

Here is an example of a script:

"Good afternoon Mr./Mrs.____. I hope I did not catch you at a bad time. I just wanted to discuss my performance over the past year. I feel that I have obtained many new skills that have been beneficial to the company. I also believe that I have been going above and beyond the call of duty and helped this organization improve in many facets. For example, I believe some of the new programs I helped to implement made this company more profitable. I want to thank you for your help in assisting me in my growth and if there is anything else I can do to improve, let me know."

Pause for feedback.

"With the extra effort and improvements I have made, I believe that I deserve extra compensation for my work. I have been a true asset to this company, and I plan to be for years to come. I believe that I have earned a higher salary of at least $10,000 extra per year."

From here, wait for there response, and thank them, whatever their answer might be.

Remember that an employee who cares about the work they do is an employee, the company wants to keep happy. Keep telling yourself that you will earn that raise and be paid what you think you are worth.

Work Overtime

If you are not able to negotiate a higher salary at this time and don't feel comfortable finding a new job, then consider working overtime. If your employer allows you to work extra hours each week, then see if you can put in the extra time to make more money. It is a win-win for everyone. Your employer can get more accomplished, and you will create more wealth.

Finding a Higher-Paying Job

If you have reached a cap in your salary with your current employer and feel like you have more to offer, then consider finding a higher paying job. I am not asking you to quit and go on a hunt. There are actually a few things you can start doing while at your current employer to make yourself more marketable to future employers. The following are some tips to find a job with higher pay.

Define the Job

The first thing you need to do is define the type of job you want, including salary. What are you earning now, and what do you expect to earn with your new employer? Take into account your commute, new benefits, and the opportunities you will have. Before you think about leaving your current role, have a clear understanding of what a better option would look like.

Leverage Your Network

Don't be shy about asking for help. What many people don't realize is that if someone helps you get hired at their company, they receive a financial incentive too. This is not always the case, but true for many companies out there. Therefore, leverage your network and put some feelers out there. Let people know you are in the market for a new job, and they might be able to point you in the right direction.

Be a Rockstar at Your Current Job

Commit yourself to be a Rockstar at your current job. Even if you are planning to leave in a few months, you want your resume to be as strong as possible. Learn new skills, be a team player, and show an unwavering work ethic. Your future employer can always contact your current employer as a reference, so you make sure they only have good things to say.

Audit Your Social Media Accounts

We don't like to believe that our employers can come across our social media accounts, but unfortunately, they can. This can end up giving them an unflattering view of who you are. Audit your social media account regularly to remove any unflattering posts and keep your personal account as private as you can.

Never Stop Building Your Resume

Your resume is often the first impression an employer will have of you. Make it a good one. There are several resume templates that you can use. Also, consider hiring a professional resume and cover letter writer. They can definitely be worth the investment if you find your dream career.

Starting a Side Hustle

This is something you literally do on the side outside of normal working hours. You can earn substantial extra income without quitting your job. The great thing about these opportunities is that they can be done at any time and from most places. You can start a side hustle to pad your income and savings. Eventually, you can turn this into a career opportunity where you become your own boss. Many individuals have used these extra opportunities to replace their full-time income, and they are happier as a result.

There are many paths to start a side hustle, and the opportunities continue to grow. Aspiring entrepreneurs can use these as a stepping-stone to financial freedom. Imagine a lifelong hobby turning into a business venture. It has happened to many people who were passionate and dedicated. If you are interested in going this route, then the following steps will help you gain some traction for your side hustle while you keep your day job as your reliable income source.

- First of all, you need to prepare for the long haul. No matter how good your product and service is, you need to have grit, determination, and a genuine interest in solving a problem. Eventually, you will start getting loyal customers, but it won't happen overnight.
- Identify your unique skills and areas of interest. Your business will only succeed in the long run if it's something you love and something you are good at. Before you start your side hustle, make sure you possess the necessary skills to do so.
- Validate your side hustle by getting a customer who is willing to pay for it. You must recognize if you are solving a real problem with your idea. If not, then it might not go anywhere. If a customer is willing to pay for your product or service, then chances are, it is solving a problem for them.
- You will have competition out there, so make sure you are differentiating yourself in some way. You need to be aware of what your competitors are doing and try to stay ahead of the curve.
- Define your goals clearly. It is not okay to just have a dream. You need concrete objectives on what you want to accomplish and by when—set milestones for yourself.
- Delegate work that is outside of your expertise. Starting up a side hustle takes a lot of work. You can't possibly focus on everything—delegate menial tasks and those that can be done better by someone else. There are freelancers out there looking for extra work, so check out sites like Upwork, Fiverr, and thumbtack.

- Ask for real customer feedback. This helps you determine how valuable your product is and what improvements need to be made.
- Don't let your focus on the side hustle take away from your day job. This is why, when you are at work, focus on work; when you are building up your side hustle, focus on that. You don't want to get fired from your job because you are focusing on your side hustle.
- Before quitting your day job, build up a sustainable flow of customers that will replace or exceed your current income.

Starting a side hustle is not easy, but the freedom and autonomy it can bring you will be worth it, especially when you have a million-dollar idea. The following are some great ideas for side hustles so you can start supplementing and increasing your income.

Selling Products on Ebay

Ebay is a great platform for earning some extra income quickly. You can start by selling things you don't use anymore. From here, you can buy products for cheap and then sell them for a profit online. For example, many people will shop at thrift stores or garage sales to find quality products for cheap, and then sell them on Ebay for a profit. You don't have to limit yourself to Ebay either. Amazon and craigslist are possible choices, too. Make sure you take quality photos of the items, so they look attractive online. Don't try to sell people junk because they can rate you online.

Drive for Uber or Lyft

This might be one of the easiest side hustles to get into. These rideshare services will allow you to transport clients to their locations, and you can work whatever hours of the day you choose. If you have a couple of hours in the morning or evening, then turn on your availability and make some extra money. If you want to spend your Saturday driving people around, you can do that, as well. Reliable transportation and a decent driving record are essential, and from here, everything is good to go. You can choose not to transport passengers and just drive for Uber Eats delivering food.

Deliver for PostMates

Similar to Uber and Lyft, you can work whenever you want during your free time. With PostMates, you can pick up and deliver food, plus earn some good tips. Other options that are similar to this are GrubHub and DoorDash. You can earn a great living in heavily trafficked cities, like New York or Los Angeles.

Sell Your Services On Fiverr

Fiverr is a great platform for freelancers who want to sell their services. If you are a professional photographer, writer, artist, musician, or trainer, you can find clients on Fiverr. Some of the top earners from Fiverr earn up to six-figures. Of course, this will take you a while.

Online Tutoring

If you have significant knowledge in a subject matter, then consider becoming a tutor online. You can use platforms like Skype or Zoom to communicate with people across the globe using video conference. This is the preferred method for many people these days due to safety issues.

Start an Air BNB Business

If you have extra space in your home or a rental property, then consider using it as an Air BNB. You can generate extra income by letting people stay temporarily in your extra space.

Dog Walking

If you have an affinity for dogs and exercise, then becoming a dog walker could be right up your alley. Many people are too busy to take their dogs for a walk and also need to go out of town for short periods. A dog walker can take these animals out to get exercise and fresh air when their owners don't have time to do so. You can obtain a lot of clientele in your neighborhood alone and make a good side income.

Mystery Shopping

Companies are looking for mystery shoppers to buy products in secret and then write about their experience. The information you provide will give companies an idea of their strengths and weaknesses.

Babysitting

If you love children, then babysitting might be right up your alley. You can make some extra money on evenings and weekends, or whenever you're available, and the client needs you. Sites like care.com and sittercity.com are great resources to find work.

Become a Personal Shopper

Do you love a good shopping experience? If so, then you might love shopping for others. Many busy professionals may not have time to go to the store, so they hire someone to go for them. You can earn some pretty good money in tips, too.

Work for Instacart

Instacart is an independent contractor platform, similar to PostMates. Their focus is on groceries. You can be a shopper or someone who picks up and delivers the groceries. Once again, you can work on your own time.

Give Music Lessons

Are you a talented musician? Consider giving lessons to students, both children, and adults, alike. You can make some great side income by doing this.

Become a Virtual Assistant

Virtual assistants are in high demand, but you have to be very organized and don't have as much freedom with your time. You have to work more on your client's schedule.

To summarize, there are many opportunities open to making extra money. Side hustling is a phenomenon that is taking over. So many individuals are getting on the train, and you can too. Consider the skills you possess and figure out how you can use them to benefit other people.

I hope you enjoyed this final chapter on how to increase your income. It takes work and persistence. There is no easy answer, but if you are willing to hustle, then the world is your oyster. Never tell yourself again that you don't deserve anything. Don't focus on cutting expenses from your life; focus on bringing in more so you can have more. You may have heard the term, "A job will never make you rich." Unfortunately, this is true unless you are making a seven-figure salary. For most of us, we need to find other avenues to generate income and become financially intelligent. If you follow the advice in this book, I am confident that you will be on your way to becoming a millionaire.

Conclusion

I want to thank all of you for taking the time to read the book, *How to Be a Millionaire*; here's hoping the material was informative and provided you with the tools you need to achieve your desired goals. Money is in abundance, but most people don't realize this. The harvest is plenty, but the workers are few, as the saying goes. However, I will not call people lazy. I simply believe they have the wrong thought process when it comes to money, which is that of a limitation mindset. It is what they grew up with because the influential adults in their lives taught them to think in this manner. My goal with this book was to change all that.

Many people dream of becoming rich, but they either don't know how or are unwilling to do what it takes. Our society believes that money is limited, and there is a scarce amount to go around. Therefore, they hold onto their wealth and never allow themselves to enjoy it. The problem is this limiting mindset impedes a person's growth and keeps them from living their full potential. Instead of figuring out ways to increase their wealth, they are hellbent on not losing their money. This prevents them from taking any risks.

When you live with a limiting mindset, instead of an abundance one, you put up a barrier between you and the rest of the world. You do not give yourself the chance to experience what is out there. Many financial gurus will teach things like, "Save every penny," "Don't spend money on that expensive cup of coffee," or "Don't buy things that you don't need." As my mentor, Remit Sethi likes to point out, if you are giving up things you love to save money, you might as well just live in a cave. What's the point of earning money if you're not going to enjoy it?

The focus of this book is not just becoming a millionaire but thinking like one too. You must stop putting limitations on yourself. You must stop telling yourself you can't afford things. When you do, you immediately shut down any chance of finding a solution. Instead, ask yourself how you can afford something, and your mind will open up to find new answers.

As I went through the chapters in this book, I discussed the many blessings of becoming rich; one of them is having the freedom and enjoying your life. After this, I went over some smart ways to get past debt, learn how to manage your finances better, and eventually increase your income. There are many paths to take before you can become a millionaire, and I tried to cover them in great detail with this book. Always remember that becoming a millionaire is an attainable goal. Start hanging around some rich people, and you will start seeing how it's done.

If you feel that some of the strategies will not make a difference, remember that becoming wealthy does multiple steps. One singular action does not change your financial situation. You must alter a variety of habits in your life.

The next step is to take the information in this book and start incorporating it into your own life. Work on changing your mindset to start thinking like a millionaire. Tear down the boundaries that exist around you so you can start living with abundance. Start paying attention to your debt and work on getting rid of it. Especially the bad debt, like credit cards. From there, work on creating the right accounts, automate your finances, increase your financial education, and start building up your wealth. You don't have to be a Wallstreet Stockbroker or run a large corporation to become a millionaire. Many wealthy individuals are just ordinary people who did extraordinary things. Start being extraordinary yourself.

The more people who learn about this book, the more I am able to help. Therefore, if you found this book beneficial, a positive review on Amazon will be greatly appreciated.

Printed in Great Britain
by Amazon